Fodor's 90
Disney World & the Orlando Area

Robert Stone

Fodor's Travel Publications, Inc.
New York and London

Fodor's Disney World & the Orlando Area

Editorial Contributor: Mike Etzkin
Art Director: Fabrizio La Rocca
Cartographer: David Lindroth
Illustrator: Karl Tanner
Cover Photograph: Jeff Foott/Bruce Colemann

Design: Vignelli Associates

Special Sales

Fodor's Travel Publications are available at special discounts for bulk purchases (100 copies or more) for sales promotions, or premiums. Special editions, including personalized covers, excerpts of existing guides, and corporate imprints, can be created in large quantities for special needs. For more information write to Special Marketing, Fodor's Travel Publications, 201 E. 50th Street, New York, NY 10022. Enquiries from the United Kingdom should be sent to Fodor's Travel Publications, 30–32 Bedford Square, London WCIB 3 SG.

Contents

Maps

Foreword

This is an exciting time for Fodor's, as we continue our ambitious program to rewrite, reformat, and redesign all 140 of our guides. Here are just a few of the new features:

★ Brand-new computer-generated maps locating all the top attractions, hotels, restaurants, and shops

★ A unique system of numbers and legends to help readers move effortlessly between text and maps

★ A new star rating system for hotels and restaurants

★ Restaurant reviews by major food critics around the world

★ Stamped, self-addressed postcards, bound into every guide, give readers a chance to help evaluate hotels and restaurants

★ Complete page redesign for instant retrieval of information

★ FODOR'S CHOICE—Our favorite museums, beaches, cafés, romantic hideaways, festivals, and more

★ HIGHLIGHTS—An insider's look at the most important developments in tourism during the past year

★ TIME OUT—The best and most convenient lunch stops along exploring routes

★ Exclusive background essays create a powerful portrait of each destination

★ A mini-journal for travelers to keep track of their own itineraries and addresses

While every care has been taken to ensure the accuracy of the information in this guide, the passage of time will always bring change, and consequently, the publisher cannot accept responsibility for errors that may occur.

All prices and opening times quoted here are based on information available to us at press time. Hours and admission fees may change, however, and the prudent traveler will avoid inconvenience by calling ahead.

Fodor's wants to hear about your travel experiences, both pleasant and unpleasant. When a hotel or restaurant fails to live up to its billing, let us know and we will investigate the complaint and revise our entries where the facts warrant it.

Send your letters to the editors of Fodor's Travel Publications, 201 E. 50th Street, New York, NY 10022.

Highlights '90 and Fodor's Choice

Highlights '90

An opportunity to see a star or be a star is the latest lure for visitors to Orlando, fast becoming Hollywood East.

When **Universal Studios Florida** opens its doors to visitors in the spring of 1990, it will be the second major film studio to do so in Orlando within a year. The Universal tour is patterned after the highly successful attraction in Los Angeles, except the Florida tours have been developed to integrate more fully the tour with studio production facilities, allowing visitors an even closer and more interactive behind-the-scenes look at movie and TV production. (See below for details on the studio's attractions.)

For visitors arriving to experience the wows of Walt's wonderland, there will be two more Disney-property hotels from which to choose. The **Dolphin** and the **Swan** will provide nearly 2,300 guest rooms, bringing the total to nearly 12,000 hotel rooms within Disney domain. Operated by Sheraton, the Dolphin will be the largest hotel on Disney grounds. Its structural highlight will be a waterfall that cascades down the face of the building into a series of seashells, and a large shellshape pool supported by four dolphin statues. The Dolphin will be connected by a landscaped walkway across the lake to the Swan, which will be run by Westin Hotels and Resorts. In typical Disney style, two 55-foot dolphins and two 47-foot swans will rise from the top of the hotels.

Away from WDW, the most significant construction has been at **Orlando International Airport,** where a third runway and terminal have been added. The expansion should be completed by June.

Among the dinner theaters in Orlando, **Medieval Times** is prospering. Raimonburg, a new village at Medieval Times, is part of a $2 million expansion project. The village features artisans in medieval settings and attire, including glassblowers, weavers, enamel craftsmen, and blacksmiths. Visitors can check out a torture chamber displaying replicas of 13th-century instruments of torture.

But the hot ticket in town for 1990 will be one to see the **Orlando Magic,** who are playing their first season in the National Basketball Association. The team plays in a new arena downtown.

The **Orlando Stadium** also will have a facelift and 20,000 new seats in time to accommodate 90,000 spectators for the Florida Citrus Bowl on New Year's Day.

Disney-MGM Studios and Universal Studios Florida

The silver screen has come to Central Florida. By mid-1990 you'll be able to explore the mystique and mechanics of the movies at two working studios just 12 miles apart from each other. One of these attractions, the **Disney-MGM Studios Theme Park** at Walt Disney World, opened to the public in 1989. The second, **Universal Studios Florida** in Orlando, is scheduled to open its doors to tourists in May 1990.

These studios decided to set up shop in Florida to take advantage of the good shooting weather, the relative proximity to New York–based talent, labor costs that undercut Hollywood's by as much as 35% and the steady supply of tourists in the area, most of whom are eager to know more about how their favorite TV shows and movies are made. Both studios produce feature films, TV shows, commercials, industrial films, and corporate audiovisual presentations. Independent filmmakers rent sound stages, office space, and post-production editing facilities at both complexes. On-site vendors and subcontractors supply cameras, sound equipment, lighting, casting services, costume rental, payroll accounting, catering, and every other conceivable product or service a producer might need.

Things to See and Do At both studios you can stroll along soundproofed corridors overlooking cavernous sound stages where movies and TV shows are produced. If your timing is right, you can even watch the filming or taping or peer into post-production areas where editors and sound technicians work.

You may also be invited to join the audience for taping a TV show. If the opportunity arises, it's best to ask whether you're guaranteed a seat or simply placed on standby; at Disney-MGM you might wait a long time and still not get a seat.

Back-lot tours promise to be popular attractions at both studios. Visitors get a chance to visit huge outdoor sets that simulate shooting locations and familiar scenes. The ride through the back lot at Disney-MGM traverses a New York cityscape and an "Anywhere U.S.A." avenue of suburban house facades (including the one where the "Golden Girls" live). Universal's back lot will offer some 50 different locations, including San Francisco's Fisherman's Wharf, 1930s Chicago, the New York waterfront, and the Bates Motel and house from *Psycho IV*.

One of the most significant differences between the two studio tours is in their approach to moving people. Disney-MGM uses a tram for much of its Backstage Studio Tour; at Universal, visitors tour the facilities on foot. The Disney-MGM tram is actually something of a mixed blessing. It provides visitors with a comfortable ride, but moves past some busy costume and scenery shops so rapidly that it's hard to take in everything.

"Thrill" rides are designed to showcase special-effects technology. In Disney-MGM's **Catastrophe Canyon** on the Backstage Studio Tour, your tram pauses at an oil field in a rocky canyon, where you are shaken and jostled by a violent earthquake. Oil tanks explode with a deafening roar, and you feel the heat. Finally, an intense thunderstorm and flash flood quench the fire. Be prepared to get wet— especially on the left side of the tram. Leaving Catastrophe Canyon, you'll see the computer-controlled technology that makes these disasters happen: a complex network of water and gas pipes, tanks with enough water to fill 10 Olympic-size swimming pools, and air cannons that shoot streams of water to create impressive effects.

Universal is planning its own earthquake (this one in San Francisco), a ride on a pontoon boat that is attacked by the killer shark from *Jaws*, and a **Kongfrontation** experience during which the 37-foot-tall ape will pick up your Roose-velt Island tram car. When a helicopter distracts Kong, he will hurl down the car, plunging you toward a nick-of-time rescue. An instant video replay will let you watch your own reactions to this monstrous adventure.

Both studios are also planning to offer strong doses of sci-fi space fantasy. Disney-MGM is collaborating with George Lucas of *Star Wars* on a **Star Tours** ride scheduled to open in the winter of 1990. It will include a visit to the Ewoks' ar-boreal village and a hair-raising light-speed trip to the Moon of Endor aboard a spacecraft with rookie droid RX-24 at the helm. This ride will employ flight-simulator technol-ogy that synchronizes your vehicle's movements with a spectacular film to make you feel what you see.

With Steven Spielberg serving as creative consultant, Uni-versal will employ similar technology to take you on a bike ride to E.T.'s home planet. You'll soar 60 feet above the San Fernando Valley, across the face of the moon, and through a purple perfume fog—to find a planet in peril. After you help E.T. save his planet, he will say goodbye to you by name. (How he will know your name is a trade secret that Universal won't reveal.) Flight-simulator technology and Spielberg's touch also will be evident in Universal's *Back to the Future* time-travel ride in Doc Brown's gull-wing car.

Visitors can also gain insights into the art of animation. At Disney-MGM you can watch films and videos that explain the tools and techniques of animation art, stroll through an elevated corridor overlooking the animation studios to watch artists at work, see film clips of animated Disney classics, and emerge through a store selling pricey posters and pricier original drawings.

Universal promises a more innovative approach to anima-tion in **The Funtastic World of Hanna-Barbera,** where an adventure experience will give you the feeling of being in-side a cartoon during a high-speed chase. You'll then learn something about the animation process and have a chance to create your own animation art.

A number of other entertaining and educational attractions are already in operation at **Disney-MGM:**

The Great Movie Ride takes you on a journey through movie history: Disney's "Animatronics" figures depict classic films of the past, and a bank robber hijacks your tram. (Note: the *Aliens* sequence may give young children nightmares.) **SuperStar Television** re-creates past TV hits, placing members of the audience on the screen with the actors. In the **Monster Sound Show** audience volunteers help audio technicians add sound effects to a creepy hauntedhouse film featuring comedian Chevy Chase. George Lucas helped Disney-MGM create the **Epic Stunt Spectacular,** a 20-minute show that demonstrates and explains a succession of elaborate action stunts. Two stops on the Backstage Studio Tour that are popular with visitors are the **Water Effects Tank**, which shows how model ships are used to make war movies and demonstrates an ocean storm scene, and the **Special Effects Workshop and Shooting Stage**, where technicians demonstrate the use of optical and mechanical effects.

Universal Studios is planning to open similar attractions in 1990:

Ghostbusters will combine live action with modern cinema technology to demonstrate and explain the ghoulish special effects from this popular film. At the **Nickelodeon Production Center**, where the Nickelodeon cable TV network tapes its shows, children will be able to watch the production, sit in the audience, and maybe even be part of the action. Lassie, Benji, Einstein from *Back to the Future*, and an assortment of horses, cats, and pigeons will appear with their trainers to demonstrate animal acting skills at the **Animal Actors Stage**. At an attraction called **Alfred Hitchcock: The Art of Making Movies**, you'll experience memorable scenes from Hitchcock's classic suspense movies, including *Psycho* and *The Birds*. In the **Murder, She Wrote Post-Production Theater** you'll assume the role of executive producer of the series: You'll get a chance to edit, select the music, and lay in the sound effects to create the final videotape. At the **Phantom of the Opera Horror Makeup Show**, artists will demonstrate the creation of horror make-up for famous characters such as the Phantom, Frankenstein's monster, and the Fly. And finally, at the **Screen Test Adventure Studio**, you'll star in your own film and get a videotape to take home.

Operating Hours At either studio, plan to arrive when the park opens—9 AM for Disney-MGM, 9:30 AM for Universal—to beat the midday mob scene. Disney-MGM covers just 135 acres, which is a relatively small area for a theme park. Universal Studios will have about 200 acres.

After the crowds thin out about 4 PM, you can enjoy a pleasant evening at Disney-MGM until closing time, which ranges from 7 to 10 PM. Universal plans to close at 6 PM for most of the year, but will stay open as late as 9 PM in peak season.

Admission A one-day ticket to Disney-MGM is $29 plus tax for adults, $23 plus tax for children age 3–10. A Four-Day All Three Parks Passport, providing admission to Disney-MGM, the Magic Kingdom, and Epcot Center on any four days, is $97 plus tax for adults, $77 plus tax for children. At press time, Universal Studios had not yet announced its prices for "studio passes."

Dining You won't starve at Disney-MGM, but don't expect the haute cuisine for which many of the restaurants in Epcot Center's World Showcase are justly famous. In addition to an assortment of fast-food restaurants offering hamburgers, hot dogs, ice cream, and soft drinks, four restaurants at the Disney-MGM complex offer more substantial fare:

The Hollywood Brown Derby, its walls lined with movie-star caricatures, features regional American cuisine and salads. The **'50s Prime Time Cafe/Tune In Lounge** looks like a 1950s kitchen, with old DuMont TV sets playing "Sgt. Bilko" and other black-and-white sitcoms of the era. Food is served on Fiesta Ware dishes and TV-dinner trays. Specialties include veal meat loaf, chili mac, and Granny's pot roast. The **Soundstage Restaurant**, on the set of the comedy film *Big Business*, is actually a food court where you line up for pizza, pasta, soups, sandwiches, and salads. Up a flight of stairs is **The Catwalk Bar**. The **Hollywood & Vine Cafeteria**, in an art-deco setting reminiscent of the '30s and '40s, features smoked baby-back ribs; grilled low-fat, low-sodium bratwurst; and rotisserie-roasted chicken with fresh herbs.

Universal Studios will be opening a **Hard Rock Cafe** that will feature American-style food and beverages, rock music, and a display of pop memorabilia that includes the baseball cap worn by Jerry Mathers in the 1957 premier of the original "Leave It to Beaver" TV series. Also planned is **Lombards Landing**, which, with 475 seats, will be the largest restaurant at Universal.

Fodor's Choice

No two people will agree on what makes a perfect vacation, but it's fun and helpful to know what others think. We hope you'll have a chance to experience some of Fodor's Choices yourself while visiting Disney World and the Orlando Area. For detailed information about each entry, refer to the appropriate chapters within this guidebook.

Lodging

Grand Cypress Resort *(Very Expensive)*

Hilton at Walt Disney World Village *(Expensive–Very Expensive)*

Peabody Orlando *(Expensive–Very Expensive)*

Disney Inn *(Expensive)*

Grand Floridian Hotel *(Expensive)*

Chalet Suzanne Country Inn *(Moderate–Expensive)*

Park Plaza Hotel *(Moderate–Expensive)*

Ramada Resort Maingate *(Moderate)*

Casa Rosa Motel *(Inexpensive)*

Dining

Alfredo's *(Expensive)*

Chalet Suzanne *(Expensive)*

Dux *(Expensive)*

Capriccio *(Moderate)*

Coq au Vin *(Moderate)*

Haifeng *(Moderate)*

Mitsukoshi *(Moderate)*

Royal Orleans *(Moderate)*

Walt Disney World

Magic Kingdom Jungle Cruise

Big Thunder Mountain Railroad

Haunted Mansion

It's a Small World

Space Mountain

Pirates of the Caribbean

Epcot: Spaceship Earth
Future World
Universe of Energy

Listen to the Land

Captain EO

Image Works

Epcot: "Wonders of China"
World Showcase "O Canada"

Outside Walt Disney World

Sea World "New Friends" (whale and dolphin show)

"Sea Lions of the Silver Screen"

"Shark Encounter"

Busch Gardens "The World of Birds"

Rollercoasters

Gatorland Zoo "Gator Jumparoo"

Off the Beaten Track

Charles Hosmer Morse Museum of American Art

Bok Tower Gardens

Cassadaga Spiritualist Camp (Sunday)

Nightlife

Mardis Gras (dinner show)

Broadway at the Top (dinner show)

Pleasure Island

Church Street Station

J.J. Whisper's

IllumiNations at Epcot Center

Shopping

Park Avenue (Winter Park)

Church Street Exchange

Mercado Mediterranean Shopping Village

World Showcase at Epcot

Bountiful Harvest, China Pavilion at Epcot

Mickey's Character Shop in WDW Shopping Village

The Florida Peninsula

GEORGIA

Amelia Island

St. Mary's R.

95 Jacksonville

ATLANTIC OCEAN

N

10

River

Osceola National Forest

St. John's River

St. Augustine

Santa Fe R.

Suwannee

41 75 Gainesville

1

301

Ocala

Ocala National Forest

40 Daytona Beach

Cedar Keys

27

4

98

19

50

50 Titusville

John F. Kennedy Space Center

Walt Disney World

Orlando

528

Cape Canaveral

Merritt Island

Tarpon Springs

75

Clearwater

Tampa

Winter Haven

4

Florida's Turnpike

Melbourne

Sebastian Inlet Recreation Area

Tampa Bay

St. Petersburg

Bradenton

Manatee R.

27

Kissimmee R.

95 Vero Beach

Fort Pierce

Sarasota

Peace R.

Hutchinson Island

Venice

75

70

Lake Okeechobee

Caloosahatchee R.

West Palm Beach

Singer Island

Cape Coral

Fort Myers

80

Palm Beach

Captiva Island

27

Sanibel Island

Boca Raton

Naples

84

Big Cypress National Preserve

Fort Lauderdale

41

Miami Beach

Gulf of Mexico

Miami

Biscayne Bay

Everglades National Park

Cape Sable

Florida Bay

0 ___ 50 miles

0 ___ 75 km

Key West

1 Florida Keys

World Time Zones

Numbers below vertical bands relate each zone to Greenwich Mean Time (0 hrs.).
Local times may differ, as indicated by lightface numbers on the map.

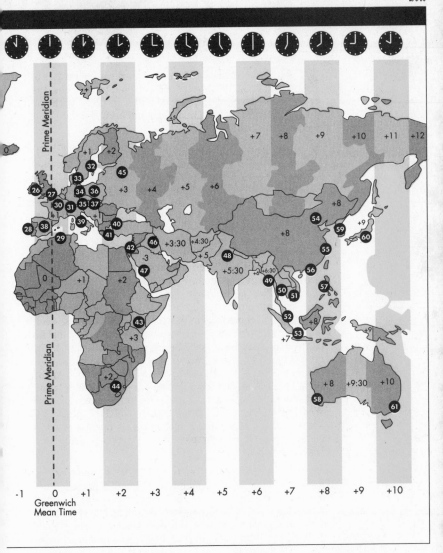

Introduction

by Karen Cure

*Ms. Cure, whose
favorite ride is
the Haunted
Mansion, writes
extensively on
Walt Disney
World.*

Millions of visitors, even those who place Pirates of the Caribbean and Space Mountain among the wonders of the world, right up there with the Eiffel Tower and the Pyramids, can't accurately define Walt Disney World.

The sheer size of the property—27,400 acres near Kissimmee, Florida—suggests that WDW is more than a single theme park, a Disneyland clone, with a fabulous castle in the center and the most dazzling rides on earth. The 27,400 acres translate to 43 square miles—twice the size of Manhattan or Bermuda, 60 times larger than Monaco, and just a shade smaller than Nantucket or Liechtenstein. If you were to drive at 60 miles per hour from one side of the property to the other, it would take close to three-quarters of an hour. On a tract that size, 98 acres is a mere speck, yet that is the size of the Magic Kingdom. When most people imagine Walt Disney World, they think only of those 98 acres, but in actuality there is much, much more. Some 2,500 acres of the 27,400 are occupied by hotels and villa complexes, each with its own theme and each equipped with recreational facilities like swimming pools and golf courses. All of these are part of Walt Disney World. Epcot Center, a little over twice the size of the Magic Kingdom, is the second major theme park. Devoted to exploring the world as it is today and may be in the future, it, too, is within the boundaries of Walt Disney World. In 1989, the Disney-MGM Studios, devoted to the doings of the film business opened nearby, along with a new villa complex. And all of that is inside Walt Disney World.

In addition, there are thousands of acres of undeveloped property—grassy plains and pine forests patrolled by deer, and swamps patched by thickets of palmettos and fluttering with white ibis—even now, almost 20 years after opening day. When you take a Walt Disney World exit off I-4 or U.S. 192 and begin traveling across empty land devoid of billboards or any other promotional materials, you're in Walt Disney World, even though there's not a Cinderella Castle in sight. It's a very, very big place.

To understand how this all came to be, it helps to go back to the beginnings of the Disney theme park organization in Anaheim, California, at Disneyland.

When it opened in 1956, amusement parks were widely considered dinosaurs of their species, a vanishing breed, cultural anachronisms. The 17th- and 18th-century European pleasure gardens where families strolled tree-lined paths between flower beds, marveled at balloon ascensions and trapeze acts, and enjoyed musical presentations—places like England's Vauxhall Gardens and Vienna's 2,000-

acre Prater, with its Ferris wheel, Russian mountains, fun houses—had given way to parks full of thrill rides. After World War II, these were abandoned by the family trade and taken over by hoodlums, staffed by sinister carnival types, and maintained poorly. What Walt Disney saw when he tried to take his daughters there were overflowing trash bins, trampled gardens, peeling paint.

While munching popcorn on a bench in one of them one day, he got the idea to build a "magical little park" for families. He persuaded his brother Roy, financial manager of his studio operation, to let him use $10,000, then borrowed on his life insurance to buy up the surrounding orange groves, and gathered a staff of "imagineers" to design the park. His colleagues and friends made gloomy predictions about what they thought of as "Walt's screwy ideas." But Disneyland, publicized on the then-nascent ABC network's weekly Disneyland show, was an instant hit, and soon the orange groves on its perimeters were sprouting motels, restaurants, and other tourist facilities, and people were traveling from all over the country to experience the phenomenon. By the end of its first decade, the number of attractions had grown from 22 to 47, the investment from $17 million to $48 million.

Walt was increasingly disturbed at the commercialization on the park's perimeter. "Believe me," he said, "if I ever build another Disneyland, I would make sure I could control the class and the theme of the enterprises around it."

At the same time, he was dreaming of a new community to show how people could live together happily in a pleasant environment.

Perhaps, he thought, a second Disneyland park would be its "weenie," the term he always used to describe something that attracted and held the interest of his visitors, the designer's answer to the carnie barker. The City of Tomorrow would be all around it. And that was how Walt Disney World developed.

As early as 1958 Walt was evaluating possible sites, and in 1959 he settled on Florida—inland Florida, away from hurricanes, salt spray, and the frivolities of the beach—and began the lengthy process of acquiring the land. The Magic Kingdom as he envisioned it, the weenie, more or less replicated the California property, with a few minor differences. As for the surrounding land, it preoccupied Disney, who called it EPCOT, an Experimental Prototype Community of Tomorrow.

In the City of Tomorrow that Disney was planning, there would be no slums, no landowning (only rentals at modest rates), no retirees (only working people). It would build upon new ideas and new technologies, and it would always be introducing, testing, and demonstrating new systems and new materials. It would be "a showcase . . . of the ingenuity and imagination of American free enterprise," and it would never be completed.

Disney himself sketched out sites of hotels, lakes, campgrounds, and entrances for visitors and service vehicles in this EPCOT, this City of Tomorrow. But in 1966, a week after plans for the "new Disneyland" were publicly announced on the Disneyland television show, he died.

His brother and partner of forty years, Roy O. Disney, carried on without him, and when the new Disney creation opened five years later he named it *Walt* Disney World in acknowledgment of the man who gave it life; among those who know the place well, the name has stuck and is never shortened to the popular "Disney World." Roy died a year later, and the company remained under the leadership of longtime Disney executives—most recently Ron Miller, the husband of Walt's daughter Diane—until 1984, when former Paramount president Michael Eisner took the helm after nine months of well-publicized takeover attempts and concomitant intramural turmoil. But as Disney himself decreed, WDW has never been completed; as one new confection is welcoming its first guests, another is beginning construction and still others are under study.

Many observers say that Epcot Center, the Disney project that opened in 1982, is merely an overblown commercial enterprise, a travesty of Walt's original vision of his EPCOT. This critique misses the point. Disney's plans to develop a ski slope on prime southern California forestland foundered on environmentalists' protests just before Epcot Center got underway, so Epcot's genesis may have had as much to do with Walt's dream as it did with a corporate cash surplus—nobody ever accused the Disney organization of being impervious to financial realities. Nonetheless, Epcot Center did turn out as the "showcase of technology" that Walt envisioned: Technology is the subject of many of the exhibits, particularly in Future World, and, more to the point, Epcot Center is state-of-the-art to its core, from the ticket-taking system to the complex computerized irrigation system, as is Walt Disney World in its entirety.

More than 15 years later, Walt Disney World still incorporates many facets of its founder's vision of a state-of-the-art settlement, an experimental prototype community of tomorrow. Though it still has no permanent residents, it does have an enormous transient population and a year-round staff numbering 20,000—more in peak periods. As a result, the Disney organization faces many of the same responsibilities that challenge the ingenuity of business and society in the outside world. And the company's distinctive responses to those challenges have earned it a reputation as an innovator.

The transportation system that serves the 43-square-mile property—buses, boats, monorail trains—manages to be decidedly pleasant as it moves millions around the property in comfort with astonishing speed. The monorail is the largest commercial transport of its kind in the world, and has moved 750 million visitors in Walt Disney World since it opened in 1971. Still, the cars look as new as the day they were built.

Utilities and other service facilities are below ground in "utilidors" so that excavations like those that pothole streets in New York and other cities are unnecessary.

Trash and waste disposal is high art, as might be expected on a property spawned by the fastidious Walt Disney (who, in Disneyland, personally patrolled the grounds in search of the single burned-out light bulb or the rare overflowing trash bin). Today at Walt Disney World, cast members from the maintenance department, in costumes appropriate to the area of WDW for which they are responsible, cover their assigned territory several times an hour. The whole system is engineered to make it easy for both staff and guests to dispose properly of trash. The ultimate receptacles are high-speed, high-tech pneumatic tubes that feed a central collection plant; the same system is now used on Roosevelt Island, off the eastern shore of Manhattan. As for waste, it's incinerated, filtered, and water-scrubbed to the point that only steam leaves the smokestack. Sewage is turned into potable water at a tertiary treatment plant or treated by ponds filled with water hyacinths, which remove the impurities; it's then used for irrigation.

In an age in which rising costs of liability insurance are shutting down municipal parks, a lesson can be learned from the safety consciousness of Disney's organization —averting accidents before they occur. Pressure-sensitive areas beneath or alongside ride vehicles in many attractions automatically shut down the system when a wayward guest gets out of the car (say, to retrieve a dropped camera). In Space Mountain, infrared cameras that can see in the dark are placed at strategic points above the tracks and monitored by a full crew, who stop the ride if any guest attempts something dangerous. The clean-swept streets are as much a matter of safety as of appearance. When accidents do occur, as is inevitable in the presence of millions of visitors a year, cast members offer a soft shoulder and then call on supervisors and security hosts, who get the facts from witnesses and the injured and write everything down. As a result, Disney hardly ever loses a personal injury case.

In employee and customer relations, the Walt Disney Company is also a leader, and was cited as such by Thomas J. Peters and Robert H. Waterman, Jr., in the best-selling *In Search of Excellence: Lessons from America's Best-Run Companies*. The Disney canon pronounces each employee a "cast member," part of the "show"; the pervasive attitude is that happy employees help make happy visitors and that bit parts are as important as starring roles. The day-long Traditions I course, part of a multiday program for new cast members, teaches about the company's history and goals and demonstrates with tours of the property how all the divisions function together to create the big show that is Walt Disney World. The organization lets cast members feel they matter in tangible ways as well. In addition to health insurance, the company pays for job-related educational programs in which cast members want to enroll and sponsors still others for college credit, organizes car pools for cast members who want them, sponsors two on-the-property child care facilities that keep the same long and unusual hours that employees themselves often do, and owns and maintains a pretty lake with beach and picnic and play areas for cast members and their families. On the job, each cast member is given the emotional support and the physical equipment he or she needs to get the job done. For instance, when the costumed characters make appearances in the park, they're accompanied by walkie-talkie-wielding colleagues in business attire—protection against the occasional over-eager guest. Finally, so that management never loses track of the challenges faced by the cast members "onstage," executives do annual "cross-utilization" stints loading rides, parking cars, serving food, and otherwise experiencing the frontline jobs. According to Peters and Waterman, such corporate emphasis on the importance of the customer and the concomitant view of the rank and file as a prime source of corporate quality and productivity are the hallmarks of America's best-run companies.

The Disney organization is equally adept at handling crowds without dehumanizing individuals. For example, Richard Schickel, author of *The Disney Version*, a thoughtful study of Walt's art and commerce, commends the handling of queues as "a marvel of technology applied to mass psychology . . . well worth the study of anybody faced with the problem of creating structures to serve large numbers of people comfortably but with no loss of efficient revenue production." The Magic Kingdom is one of "the most intelligently conceived pieces of architecture in America." Many queues snake through rope-and-stanchion mazes arranged so as to provide a changing view of humanity and keep guests entertained; when lines are particularly long, strolling entertainers are dispatched. In the Magic Kingdom's Big Thunder Mountain Railroad and Space Mountain, the queue is part of the show: To establish just the right mood, the line at the former snakes between reddish man-made boulders fuzzed by real desert plants, past a rushing stream, and underneath the tracks at a point at which all aboard are squealing with mixed terror and delight; inside Space Mountain, where all is dark, waiting passengers can only speculate on the cause of the screams as they watch the "shooting stars" and "meteorites" overhead and listen to the rumbling and clattering of the "rockets" on the tracks. The suspense is exquisite. Throughout WDW, footpaths are wide enough for crowds but seem intimate as well because they're seldom straight-as-an-arrow. The curves set the tone for a visit: They suggest strolling and, by design, encourage guests to slow down and smell the flowers. And when eager visitors both young and old race pell-mell to their favorite attraction after a theme park's morning opening, you can't help but think of pressured Manhattan executives racing for a rush-hour subway car before the doors close; the whole scene seems curiously at odds with the environment, which is one of ease, relaxation, pleasure.

Walt Disney's City of Tomorrow, a community where people would actually live, still does not exist per se; even now it is no farther than the discussion stages, and the Epcot Center that now exists is still only a *center*, a focal point. But Walt Disney World as a whole has evolved as an experimental community that is very close to Walt's dream; and the visual representations of future communities as seen in Future World's Horizons pavilion and the light-spangled model city-in-the-dark in World of Motion are less to the point than how it feels to work at Disney or to be a guest of the Disney organization in one of its theme parks or hotels.

No matter which point of view you take, the place is very grand. From the gardens full of birds and butterflies, bamboo thickets and topiary statues, to the lakes thrumming with motorboats and the shops brimming over with treasures and trinkets that sometimes seem irresistible, every detail is as highly polished as a Disney film. In the hotels, wake-up calls come when they're supposed to, room-service breakfasts are delivered on time with no missing pieces, and at the end of a visit the bill appears under the door; if it's accurate, you don't even need to check out. The Disney experience swings between poles—the sheer fun of the Magic Kingdom or of song-and-dance shows like Fort Wilderness' Hoop-Dee-Doo-Revue to the interesting and handsomely presented displays of Epcot Center, which is informative enough not to bore but never so intellectually taxing that you forget you're on vacation. There is plenty of music everywhere, and it's nearly always tuneful. (You can just imagine Walt saying to the bandleader, as he once did in Disneyland, "I don't want to hear you playing anything that I can't walk away humming.") The stray gum wrapper on the sidewalk always comes as a surprise. You can relax, stop fighting the battles of life in the real world, and let yourself be seduced by the prettiness and pleasantness of it all.

Only after the thrill and the novelty of it all wears off do you begin to wonder, "So what? What about the crises of cities today? Can Mickey Mouse transform the slums, educate the disadvantaged, repair rifts in drug-torn families, solve the crisis in health care aggravated by AIDS?" Walt himself once declined a suggestion, by science fiction author Ray Bradbury, that he run for mayor of Los Angeles. Why should I run for mayor, Walt is reported to have said, when I'm already king?

In fact, the very desire to create a Disneyland or a Walt Disney World suggests he knew how hard it would be to control complex issues in the real world. It may be that Walt was not thinker enough to grapple with them. Or it may be that he never meant to address them at all, at least at Walt Disney World; that he intended simply to sketch a direction for the future in the broadest possible strokes and to structure a situation in which certain new technologies could have their day in the sun.

Certainly, on those terms, Walt Disney World is a great success. Visiting any portion of Walt Disney World, you can't help but wish that more airlines, government agencies, and other organizations that serve the public did the job as well as WDW, that more of them equated public safety and cleanliness with profits, that more employers would even give lip service to making their employees feel appreciated, or, even better, that they understood that good employee relations can be good business.

In the meantime, as you take a heart-stopping swoop through the star-glittering galaxy of the Magic Kingdom's Space Mountain, or, in Epcot Center, sit under the shade of a Callary pear tree frosted with blooms, or inspect the rose gardens flourishing in the shadow of Canada, or watch the gyrations of the belly dancer's belly in the cool Moroccan courtyard, or gasp at yet another massive explosion of unbelievable pyrotechnics in the new IllumiNations fireworks show, the pleasure of the moment is more than enough.

1 Essential Information

Before You Go

Visitor Information

Visitors to Mickey's realm should direct all inquiries to **Walt Disney World,** Box 10000, Lake Buena Vista, FL 32830. Attention: Guest letters. Tel. 407/824–4321. Request a free copy of the *Walt Disney World Vacation Guide.* For accommodations, *see* Lodging chapter.

For information on the Greater Orlando area, contact the **Tourist Information Center,** 8445 International Dr., Orlando, FL 32819, tel. 407/363–5800. Open daily 8–8. Ask for the free *Discover Orlando* guidebook.

Visitors to the Kissimmee area on U.S. 192 can get brochures from the **Kissimmee/St. Cloud Convention and Visitors' Bureau,** 1925 E. Spacecoast Hwy. E., U.S. 192, Kissimmee, FL, 32742, tel. 407/363–5800; in FL 800/432–9199, outside FL 800/327–9159.

Tour Groups

The vast majority of Disney-bound travelers opt for independent rather than group packages. With so many rental cars and buses to and from Orlando attractions, getting around is easy enough on your own. Choosing a package will depend mostly on your pocketbook. As a general rule, the farther the hotel is from Disney's front door, the less expensive it will be. Quality ranges from roadside motels to gleaming new resort-style hotels—as usual, you get what you pay for.

When considering a tour, be sure to find out (1) exactly what expenses are included, particularly tips, taxes, sidetrips, additional meals, and entertainment; (2) ratings of all hotels on the itinerary and the facilities they offer; (3) cancellation policies for both you and for the tour operator; and (4) if you are traveling alone, what the single supplement is. Most tour operators request that bookings be made through a travel agent—there is no additional charge for doing so.

General-Interest Tours

Cosmos/Globus Gateway (150 S. Los Robles Ave., Suite 860, Pasadena, CA 91101, tel. 818/449–0919 or 800/556–5454) offers a comprehensive eight-day tour that includes entry to Disney World and Epcot Center. If you live in the eastern half of the country, **Domenico Tours** (751 Broadway, Bayonne, NJ 07002, tel. 800/554–TOUR) will take you to Orlando via coach tour or direct flight; from the West it's air only.

Package Deals for Independent Travelers

American Express Vacations (Box 5014, Atlanta, GA 30302, tel. 800/637–6200, or in GA 800/282–0800) gives you a choice of over a dozen hotels (at a wide range of prices) in its independent packages, some at WDW Village Hotel Plaza (on Disney World property, but not in Disney-owned hotels), others in nearby areas. **American Fly AAway Florida** (tel. 800/433–7300 or 817/355–1234) offers some packages to Florida, including admission to Sea World, but not Walt Disney World. **Eastern Airlines** (tel. 800/545–1400) has numerous packages, some with car rental, most with admission to the Magic Kingdom and/or Epcot Center. Eastern also lets you combine a Disney package with any of its many other Florida packages. **Delta Air Lines** (tel. 800/221–6666 or 404/765–2952) packages put you in Disney-owned hotels, with a three- or five-day pass and choice of midsize car rental or free transfers. **Firstours** (12755 State Highway 55, Minneapolis, MN 55441, tel. 612/540–5000 or 800/556–5660) offers accommodations and car rental or transfers, but you have to buy Disney and Epcot passes yourself.

Tips for British Travelers

Tourist Offices Direct inquiries to **Walt Disney Co.** (31–32 Soho Sq., London W1V 6AP, tel. 01/734–8111).

For travel outside Disney World, contact the **U. S. Travel and Tourism Administration** (2 Sackville St., London W1X 2EA, tel. 01/439–7433).

Passports and Visas You will need both a passport (cost £15) and a U.S. Visitor's Visa. The visa is available either from your travel agent or by post from the U.S. Embassy, Visa and Immigration Dept., 5 Upper Grosvenor St., London W1A 2JB, tel. 01/499–3443. The embassy no longer accepts visa applications in person. No vaccinations are required for entry into the USA.

Customs Visitors 21 and over can take in 200 cigarettes *or* 50 cigars *or* 3 lbs. of tobacco; 1 liter of alcohol; and duty-free gifts to a value of $100. Don't try to take in meat or meat products, seeds, plants, fruits, etc. Avoid illegal drugs like the plague.

Returning to Britain you can bring home: (1) 200 cigarettes *or* 100 cigarillos *or* 50 cigars *or* 250 grams of tobacco; (2) two liters of table wine with additional allowances for (a) one liter of alcohol over 22% by volume (most spirits), (b) two liters of alcohol under 22% by volume (fortified or sparkling wine), or (c) two more liters of table wine; (3) 50 grams of perfume and ¼ liter of toilet water; and (4) other goods up to a value of £32.

Insurance We recommend that you insure yourself against sickness and motoring mishaps with **Europ Assistance**, 252 High St., Croydon, Surrey CR0 1NF, tel. 01/680–1234. It is also wise to take out insurance to cover lost luggage (though check to see whether you are already covered through your existing homeowner's policy) and trip cancellation. The **Association of British Insurers** (Aldermary House, Queen St., tel. 01/248–4477) will give comprehensive advice on all aspects of vacation insurance.

Tour Operators Among the many companies offering packages to Disney World and the Orlando area are:

American Airplan (Airplan House, Churchfield Rd., Walton-on-Thames, Surrey KT12 2TJ, tel. 0932/246166).

Jetlife Holidays (169–171 High St., Orpington, Kent BR6 0LW, tel. 0689/77061) offers 14-day Orlando vacations ranging from £459 to £1199 depending on hotel and season. The price includes free car hire with unlimited mileage.

Kuoni Travel (Kuoni House, Dorking, Surrey RH5 4AZ, tel. 0306/740500) has seven-night vacations from £475 to £580. They add a rented car for £10 per person to the bargain.

Sovereign Holidays (Groundstar House, London Road, Crawley, RH10 2TB, tel. 0293/561444) offers packages for seven days from £679.

Thomas Cook Holidays (Thorpe Wood, Box 36, Peterborough, Cambridgeshire PE3 6SB, tel. 0733–63200).

When to Go

Timing is critical; choosing the right time can spell the difference between a good vacation and a great one. On certain days of the year the parks are so packed and the lines so long that you may have time for only a few rides. Then there are many more days when the lines are insignificant.

The first thing to remember is that the busiest days of the week in the Magic Kingdom are Monday, Tuesday, and Wednesday. You would think the weekend would be busiest, but it's not. Perhaps everyone tries to beat the crowds by going in the early part of the week; or perhaps vacationers leave work on Friday, travel over the weekend, and begin their visits on Monday. Whatever the reason, Friday and Sunday are the slowest days of the week, and Thursdays and Saturdays are only moderately busy.

The best times of day to be at the parks are first thing in the morning (until 11) and in the early and late evening—especially during summer months and holidays when the attractions stay open late.

The most crowded time of the year is from Christmas through New Year's Day. If you hate crowds, avoid this week like the plague. The parks are also packed around Easter. Memorial Day weekend is not only crowded, but temperatures can be quite high. The thought of standing in an hour-long line in humid 90-degree heat should be enough to dissuade you from going then. Other inadvisable times of the year are from mid-June through mid-August, Thanksgiving weekend, the week of Washington's Birthday in mid-February, and the weeks of college spring break in late March.

The rest of the year is generally hassle-free, particularly from early September until just before Thanksgiving. The best time of all is from just after the Thanksgiving weekend until the beginning of the Christmas holidays. Another excellent time is from early January through the first week of February. If you must go during summer, late August is best.

It is a good idea to stay in the most convenient property you can afford. That way, you can start out bright and early, when the parks aren't too crowded, go back to your hotel at midday when they begin to get congested, and return to the parks after dinner, when the crowds will have thinned out considerably.

Climate The following are average daily maximum and minimum temperatures for Orlando.

Jan.	70F	21C	May	88F	31C	Sept.	88F	31C
	49	9		67	19		74	23
Feb.	72F	22C	June	90F	32C	Oct.	83F	28C
	54	12		74	23		67	19
Mar.	76F	24C	July	90F	32C	Nov.	76F	24C
	56	13		74	23		58	14
Apr.	81F	27C	Aug.	90F	32C	Dec.	70F	21C
	63	17		74	23		52	11

Current weather information on 235 cities around the world—180 of them in the United States—is only a phone call away. To obtain the **Weather Trak** telephone number for your area, call 800/247–3282. The local number plays a taped message that tells you to dial a three-digit access code for the destination you're interested in. The code is either the area code (in the United States) or the first three letters of the foreign city. For a list of all access codes, send a stamped, self-addressed envelope to Cities, Box 7000, Dallas, TX 75209. For further information, phone 214/556–1122 or 800/247–3282.

Festivals and Seasonal Events

Top seasonal events at Disney World and in the Orlando area include the Florida Citrus Bowl on New Year's Day, the Walt Disney World Wine Festival in February, Light Up Orlando in the fall, and the Disney World Halloween and Christmas celebrations. For exact dates and further details about the following events, contact the **Orlando/Orange County Convention and Visitors Bureau,** Inc. (8445 International Dr., Orlando, FL 32819, tel. 407/363–5800), or **Walt Disney World** (Box 40, Lake Buena Vista, FL 32830, tel. 407/824–4321).

Jan. 1: Florida Citrus Bowl Football Classic takes place at Orlando Stadium. Tel. 407/423–2476.
Mid-Jan.: Scottish Highland Games are played at Orlando's Central Florida Fairgrounds. Tel. 407/422–8226.
Early Feb.: Walt Disney World Village Wine Festival includes 60 participating wineries from all over the country. Tel. 407/824–4531.
Late Feb.–early Mar.: Central Florida Fair is held annually at the Central Florida Fairgrounds in Orlando. Tel. 407/295–3247.
Early–late Mar.: Houston Astros Spring Training at Osceola County Stadium in Kissimmee. Tel. 407/933–5500.
Early–late Mar.: Minnesota Twins Spring Training is at Tinker Field in Orlando. Tel. 407/849–6346.
Early–late Mar.: Kansas City Royals Spring Training is at Baseball City Stadium at Boardwalk & Baseball. Tel. 813/648–5151.
Mar. 17: St. Patrick's Day Street Party encourages the wearin' o' the green at Church Street Station. Tel. 407/422–2434.
Mid Mar.: Nestle Invitational is a regular Professional Golfers Association tour stop at Bay Hill Club in Orlando. Tel. 407/876–2888.
Easter Sunday: Easter Sunrise Service is presented at the Atlantis Theatre at Sea World, 7007 Sea World Drive, Orlando 32821, tel. 407/351–3600.
Late May: Annual "Up, Up and Away" Airport Art Show takes place at Orlando International Airport. Tel. 407/826–2055.

Late June–Early July: Silver Spurs Rodeo is held in Kissimmee. Tel. 407/847–5000.

Sept.: Oktoberfest includes oompah bands, German folk dancers, German food and beer at Church Street Station. Tel. 407/422–2434.

Mid-Oct.: Walt Disney World PGA Golf Tournament is played on the three Walt Disney World 18-hole golf courses. Tel. 407/824–2250.

Late Oct.: Pioneer Days Folk Festival includes craftspeople and musicians at the Center Grounds on Randolph Street in Pine Castle. Tel. 407/855–7461.

Oct. 31: Halloween Street Party is held at Church Street Station. Tel. 407/422–2434.

Oct. 31: Halloween Party at Walt Disney World Village is a colorful, costumed event. Tel. 407/828–3425.

Mid-Nov.: Festival of the Masters is an art festival with works by 230 top artists held at Walt Disney World Village. Tel. 407/828–3425.

Mid-Nov.: Light Up Orlando is a street party downtown with live entertainment. Tel. 407/648–4010.

Early Dec.: Pet Fair is held in Orlando's Loch Haven Park. Tel. 407/896–7151.

Early Dec.: Annual Half Marathon begins in Lake Eola Park in downtown Orlando. Tel. 407/423–2476.

Dec.: Glory and Pageantry of Christmas Nativity Scene is at Walt Disney World Village. Tel. 407/828–3425.

Dec. 31: Citrus Bowl Parade takes place in Orlando. Tel. 407/423–2476.

What to Pack

Winters are mild in Orlando and summers are hot and humid. Daytime temperatures in the winter months average in the 70s and low 80s, but evening temperatures can dip to the 60s, so take a sweater or jacket, just in case. Year round, be prepared for air-conditioning bordering on the glacial. Orlando and Disney World are extremely casual, day and night. Men will need a jacket and tie for only a handful of restaurants. Casual resortwear is the norm elsewhere. For sightseeing and visits to Disney World, pack walking shorts, sundresses, cotton slacks, and T-shirts. Comfortable walking shoes or sneakers are essential. Pack an umbrella for sudden thunderstorms during the summer, but leave the plastic raincoats behind, they're extremely uncomfortable in the high humidity. In the summer, you'll want a sun hat and plenty of sunscreen lotion, even for strolls in the city, because the sun can be fierce.

Cash Machines

Virtually all U.S. banks belong to a network of ATMs (Automatic Teller Machines) that dispense cash 24 hours a day in cities throughout the country. There are some eight major networks in the USA, the largest of which are Cirrus, owned by MasterCard, and Plus, affiliated with Visa. Some banks belong to more than one network. These cards are not automatically issued; you have to apply for them. Cards issued by Visa and MasterCard also may be used in the ATMs, but the fees are usually higher than the fees on bank cards. There is also a daily interest charge on credit card "loans," even if monthly bills are paid on time. Each network has a toll-free number you can call to locate machines in a given city. The Cirrus number is 800/4–CIRRUS; the Plus number is 800/THE–PLUS. Check with your bank for information on fees and on the amount of cash you can withdraw on any given day.

Traveling with Film

If your camera is new, shoot and develop a few rolls before leaving home. Pack some lens tissue and an extra battery for your built-in light meter. Invest about $10 in a skylight filter and screw it onto the front of your lens. It will protect the lens and also reduce haze.

Film doesn't like hot weather. If you're driving in summer, don't store film in the glove compartment or on the shelf under the rear window. Put it behind the front seat on the floor, on the side opposite the exhaust pipe.

On a plane trip, never pack unprocessed film in check-in luggage; if your bags get X-rayed, you can say goodbye to your pictures. Always carry undeveloped film with you through security and ask to have it inspected by hand. (It helps to isolate your film in a plastic bag, ready for quick inspection.) Inspectors at American airports are required by law to honor requests for hand inspection; abroad, you'll have to depend on the kindness of strangers.

The old airport scanning machines—still in use in some Third World countries—use heavy doses of radiation that can turn a family portrait into an early morning fog. The newer models—used in all U.S. airports—are safe for anything from five to 500 scans, depending on the speed of your film. The effects are cumulative; you can put the same roll of film through several scans without worry. After five scans, though, you're asking for trouble.

If your film gets fogged and you want an explanation, send it to the **National Association of Photographic Manufacturers,** (600 Mamaroneck Ave., Harrison, NY 10528). They will try to determine what went wrong. The service is free.

Car Rentals

It is by no means absolutely necessary to rent a car when you are in Orlando. Just about every hotel, and even many motels, are linked to one of several private transportation systems that shuttle travelers back and forth to most of the area attractions for only a few dollars. And if you are staying at a Disney hotel, or purchase a Passport (3 or more days) instead of daily tickets, your transportation within Disney World is free.

Should you want to visit some of the less frequented attractions outside of Disney World, however, or dine in restaurants that are off the beaten tourist track, then a rental car is essential. Keep in mind that public transportation in Orlando is practically nonexistent. As for taxi cabs, try not to think about them unless you're going a short distance. Everything in Orlando is spread out and hopping in a cab every time you want to go someplace may put you on an expressway to the poorhouse.

Fortunately, Orlando offers some of the lowest rental car rates in the entire United States—not what you would expect from one of the tourist capitals of the world. The secret is to rent at special weekly rates and not return the car before the week is up. If you keep a car less than seven days, be prepared to pay daily rates—which can cost twice as much as weekly rates. It's the sort of promotional gimmickry for which car rentals companies are infamous.

When renting, be sure to consider taking out Collision Damage Waiver (CDW) insurance. It costs a few dollars more but is usually worth it, because even the smallest fender-bender can be outrageously expensive. Your own car insurance policy may cover rentals, but you will have to advance the cost of damage until the claim is settled, which can deplete your supply of cash or exceed the limit on your credit card.

Many car rental companies have counters in the major hotels and on Level 2 of the Orlando Airport. Companies with offices in Orlando or near, but not actually in, the airport, have rates that are generally lower. These budget firms usually have free pickup service at the hotels and outside the airport.

Orlando International Airport **Alamo** (tel. 800/327–9633).
Avis (tel. 800/331–1212).
Budget (tel. 800/527–0700).
Dollar (tel. 800/421–6868).
Hertz (tel. 800/654–3131).
National (tel. 800/328–4567).
Thrifty (tel. 800/367–2277).

Traveling with Children

All hotels on Disney property have playgrounds and game rooms with pinball machines and video games. Both the Polynesian Village and the Contemporary Resort have child-care facilities. All guests in the Orlando area can make use of the preschool and day-care facilities at Walt Disney World. *Children from 6 months to 12 years are accepted Mon.–Sat., 6 AM–10 PM and Sun., 6 AM–9 PM. Tel. 407/827–KIDS.*

If you're worried about your children getting lost, get them name tags either at the Magic Kingdom (at City Hall or at the Baby Center next to the Crystal Palace) or at Epcot Center (at Earth Station or the Baby Care Center).

If your children do get lost, check the lost children's logbooks in either the Baby Care Center or City Hall in the Magic Kingdom; or in either the Earth Station or the Baby Care Center behind the Odyssey Restaurant in Epcot Center.

Strollers may be rented at the Stroller Shop near the entrance to the Magic Kingdom (on the east side of Main St.), or at the French pavilion at Epcot Center.

Both the Magic Kingdom and Epcot Center have Baby Care Centers with facilities for changing infants and preparing formulas. Baby food, pacifiers, and disposable diapers can be purchased here. Travelers not staying on Disney property can make baby-sitting arrangements with the hotel concierge or housekeeper, or by contacting **Fairy Godmother's Child Care** (tel. 407/277–3724).

Breakfasts Kids love these daily breakfasts, where they can hold hands with and give bear hugs to all the best-loved Disney characters

—Mickey, Minnie, Goofy, Donald, and others. Mickey and his friends appear all morning at Contemporary Resort and Polynesian Village Resort, as well as at the Empress Lilly Showboat and Buena Vista Palace in Walt Disney World Village. A completely different character show called "Chip and Dale's Country Morning Jamboree," featuring Melvin the Moose, takes place at the Fort Wilderness Resort. The price of these buffet breakfasts varies from place to place. Unless otherwise listed, call W–DISNEY. *Contemporary Resort, Terrace Cafe, 8–11 AM. Polynesian Village, Papeete Bay Verandah, 7:40–10:30 AM. Fort Wilderness Resort, Pioneer Hall; shows at 8 and 9:45 AM. Empress Lilly, appearances at 9 and 10:30 AM. Buena Vista Palace Hotel, tel. 407/827–2727; Sun. only, 8–10:30 AM. Grand Floridian Cafe, tel. 407/824–2383; 7–10 AM.*

In all but the smallest motels there is little or no charge for children under 18 who share a room with an adult.

Publications *Family Travel Times* is an 8- to 12-page newsletter published 10 times a year by TWYCH (Travel with Your Children), 80 Eighth Ave., New York, NY 10011, tel. 212/206–0688. Subscription includes access to back issues and twice-weekly opportunities to phone for specific advice.

Getting There On domestic flights, children under 2 not occupying a seat travel free. Various discounts apply to children 2–12. Reserve a seat behind the bulkhead of the plane, which offers more leg room and can usually fit a bassinet (supplied by the airline). At the same time, inquire about special children's meals or snacks, offered by most airlines. (See "TWYCH's Airline Guide" in the February 1988 issue of *Family Travel Times* for a rundown on the services offered by 46 airlines.) Ask in advance if you can bring aboard your child's car seat. For the booklet "Child/ Infant Safety Seats Acceptable for Use in Aircraft," write Community and Consumer Liaison Division, APA–200 Federal Aviation Administration, Washington, DC 20591, tel. 202/267–3479.

Hints for Older Travelers

The American Association of Retired Persons (AARP, 1909 K St., NW, Washington, DC 20049, tel. 202/662–4850) has two programs for independent travelers: (1) *The Purchase Privilege Program*, which offers discounts on hotels, airfare (American Airlines only), car rentals, and sightseeing; and (2) the *AARP Motoring Plan*, which offers emergency aid and trip routing information for an annual fee of $29.50 per couple. AARP members must be 50 or older. Annual dues are $5 per person or per couple.

When using an AARP or other identification card, ask for a reduced hotel rate when you make your reservation, not when you check out. At restaurants, show your card to the maitre d' before you are seated, since discounts may be limited to certain set menus, days, or hours. When renting a car, remember that economy cars priced at promotional rates may cost less than cars that are available with your ID card.

Travel Industry and Disabled Exchange (TIDE, 5435 Donna Ave., Tarzana, CA 91356, tel. 818/343–6339) is an industry-based organization with a $15 per person annual membership fee. Members receive a quarterly newsletter and information on travel agencies and tours.

National Council of Senior Citizens (925 15th St., NW, Washington, DC 20005, tel. 202/347–8800) is a nonprofit advocacy group with some 4,000 local clubs across the country. Annual membership is $12 per person or $16 per couple. Members receive a monthly newspaper with travel information and an ID card for reduced rates on hotels and car rentals. The council runs frequent tours to Disney World.

Mature Outlook (6001 N. Clark St., Chicago, IL 60660, tel. 800/336–6330), a subsidiary of Sears Roebuck & Co., is a travel club for people over 50, with hotel and motel discounts and a bi-monthly newsletter. Annual membership is $9.95 per couple. Instant membership is available at participating Holiday Inns.

Golden Age Passport is a free lifetime pass to all parks, monuments, and recreation areas run by the federal government. People over 62 should pick them up in person at any national park that charges admission. A driver's license or other proof of age is required.

September Days Club is run by the moderately priced Days Inns of America (tel. 800/241–5050). The $12 annual membership fee for individuals or couples over 50 entitles them to reduced car rental rates and reductions of 15–50% at some 95% of the chain's more than 350 motels.

Greyhound (tel. 800/531–5332) and **Amtrak** (tel. 800/USA-RAIL) offer special fares for senior citizens. Amtrak has a free access guide.

Travel Tips for Senior Citizens (U.S. Dept. of State Publication 8970, revised Sept. 1987) is available for $1 from the Superintendent of Documents, U.S. Government Printing Office, Washington, DC 20402.

The Senior Citizen's Guide to Budget Travel in the United States and Canada is available for $4.95, including postage, from Pilot Books (103 Cooper St., Babylon, NY 11702, tel. 516/422–2225).

The Discount Guide for Travelers over 55, by Caroline and Walter Weintz (Dutton, $7.95), lists helpful addresses, package tours, reduced-rate car rentals, etc., in the USA and abroad.

Hints for Disabled Travelers

A free booklet, "The Disabled Guest," is available from Disney World (Box 10000, Lake Buena Vista, FL 32830, tel. 407/827–7090). Facilities are extensive, including wheelchair rentals near the entrances to both the Magic Kingdom and Epcot.

The Information Center for Individuals with Disabilities (20 Park Plaza, Room 330, Boston, MA 02116, tel. 617/727–5540) offers useful problem-solving assistance, including lists of travel agents that specialize in tours for the disabled.

Moss Rehabilitation Hospital Travel Information Service (12th St. and Taber Rd., Philadelphia, PA 19141, tel. 215/456–9900) provides information on tourist sights, transportation, and accommodations in destinations around the world. The fee is $5 for information on up to three destinations. Allow one month for delivery.

Mobility International (Box 3551, Eugene, OR 97403, tel. 503/343–1284) has information on accommodations, organized study, etc., around the world.

The Society for the Advancement of Travel for the Handicapped

(26 Court St., Brooklyn, NY 11242, tel. 718/858-5483) offers access information. Annual membership costs $40, or $25 for senior travelers and students. Send a stamped, self-addressed envelope.

Greyhound (tel. 800/531-5332) will carry a disabled person and companion for the price of a single fare. **Amtrak** (tel. 800/USA-RAIL) requests 24-hour notice to provide redcap service, special seats, and a 25% discount.

The Itinerary (Box 1084, Bayonne, NJ 07002, tel. 201/858-3400) is a bimonthly travel magazine for the disabled.

Access to the World: A Travel Guide for the Handicapped by Louise Weiss is useful but out of date; available from Facts on File (460 Park Ave. S., New York, NY 10016, tel. 212/683-2244). *Frommer's Guide for Disabled Travelers* is also useful but dated.

Further Reading

Still the most perceptive book on Disney is *The Disney Version* (1985 edition) by Richard Schickel. Disney's art is featured in *Disneyland: Inside Story*, by Randy Bright, a $35 art book published by Harry N. Abrams. Much of the action in Tom Wolfe's *The Right Stuff* (1984) takes place at Cape Canaveral, near Orlando. For a good read about Disney and other animators, look for *Of Mice and Magic* (1987) by Leonard Maltin. *Walt Disney: An American Original* by Bob Thomas is full of anecdotes about the development of WDW.

Arriving and Departing

By Plane

More than 33 scheduled airlines operate in and out of the airport, with direct service to more than 50 U.S. cities as well as to major cities in Europe, South America, Mexico, and Canada. At last count, Delta, the official airline of Disney World, had 56 flights daily to and from Orlando. Travel packages to Disney World are offered by Delta (tel. 800/221-1212) and Pan Am (tel. 800/221-1111). When booking reservations, keep in mind the distinction between nonstop flights (no stops and no changes), direct flights (no changes of aircraft, but one or more stops), and connecting flights (one or more changes of planes at one or more stops). Connecting flights are often the least expensive, but they are the most time-consuming, and the biggest nuisance.

Major U.S. airlines that serve Orlando include American, Braniff, British Airways, Continental, Delta, Eastern, Icelandair, KLM, Midway, Northwest, Pan Am, Piedmont, TWA, United, and USAir.

The Orlando Airport has a Disney World information booth where tickets, maps, and information are available. Buying tickets here while waiting for your bags to be off-loaded will save time later on.

Smoking If cigarette smoke bothers you, request a seat *far away from* the smoking section. Remember, FAA regulations require airlines to find seats for all nonsmokers.

Carry-on Luggage Under new rules in effect since January 1988, passengers are usually limited to two carry-on bags. For bags stored under your seat, the maximum dimensions are 9″ × 14″ × 22″, a total of 45″. For bags that can be hung in a closet, the maximum dimensions are 4″ × 23″ × 45″, a total of 72″. For bags stored in an overhead bin, the maximum dimensions are 10″ × 14″ × 36″, a total of 60″. Any item that exceeds the specified dimensions will generally be rejected as a carry-on, and handled as checked baggage. Keep in mind that an airline can adapt these rules to circumstances, so on an especially crowded flight don't be surprised if you are allowed only one carry-on bag.

In addition to the two bags, passengers may also carry aboard: a handbag (pocketbook or purse), an overcoat or wrap, an umbrella, a camera, a reasonable amount of reading material, an infant bag, crutches, cane, braces, or other prosthetic device upon which the passenger is dependent, and an infant/child safety seat.

Note that these regulations are for U.S. airlines only. Foreign airlines generally allow one piece of carry-on luggage in tourist class, in addition to handbags and bags filled with duty-free goods. Passengers in first and business class are also allowed to carry on one garment bag. It is best to check with your airline ahead of time to find out what their exact rules are regarding carry-on luggage.

Certain toy guns, toy knives, etc., sold in Frontierland and Adventureland should be packed in checked luggage. Security may give you a hard time if you try to carry them on board.

Checked Luggage U.S. airlines allow passengers to check in two suitcases whose total dimensions (length + width + height) do not exceed 60″. There are no weight restrictions on these bags.

Rules governing foreign airlines vary from airline to airline, so check with your travel agent or the airline itself before you go. All the airlines allow passengers to check in two bags. In general, expect the weight restriction on the two bags to be not more than 70 lbs. each, and the size restriction on the first bag to be 62″ total dimensions, and on the second bag 55″ total dimensions.

Lost Luggage On domestic flights, airlines are responsible for lost or damaged property only up to $1,250 per passenger. If you're carrying valuables, either take them with you on the airplane or purchase additional insurance for lost luggage. Some airlines will issue additional luggage insurance when you check in, but many do not. Insurance for lost, damaged, or stolen luggage is available through travel agents or directly through various insurance companies. Two that issue luggage insurance are **Tele-Trip** (tel. 800/228–9792), a subsidiary of Mutual of Omaha, and **The Travelers Insurance Co.** (Ticket and Travel Dept., 1 Tower Sq., Hartford, CT 06183, tel. 800/243–0191). Tele-Trip operates sales booths at airports, and also issues insurance through travel agents. Tele-Trip will insure checked luggage for up to 180 days and for $500 to $3,000 valuation. Rates vary from state to state. The Travelers Insurance Co. will insure checked or hand luggage from $500 to $2,000 valuation per person, and also for a maximum of 180 days. Rates for 1–5 days for $500 valuation are $10; for 180 days, $85.

Other companies with comprehensive policies include **Access America Inc.**, a subsidiary of Blue Cross-Blue Shield (Box 807, New York, NY 10163, tel. 800/851–2800) and **Near, Inc.** (1900 N. MacArthur Blvd., Suite 210, Oklahoma City, OK 73127, tel. 800/654–6700).

Before you go, itemize the contents of each bag in case you need to file an insurance claim. Be certain to put your home address on each piece of luggage, including carry-on bags. If your luggage is stolen and later recovered, the airline must deliver the luggage to your home free of charge.

Between the Airport and the Hotels There are several shuttle and limousine services at the airport that offer regularly scheduled service (as well as charter service) to and from many major hotels, leaving every half-hour to Disney properties and every hour to less busy destinations. Ticket counters are in the baggage claim area. When making hotel reservations, check to see if your hotel offers free shuttle service from the airport. If not, ask for the name of the service that is most convenient.

By Bus You can catch a public bus between the airport and downtown Orlando, which goes to and from the main terminal of the **Tri-County Transit Authority** (438 Woods Ave., Orlando, tel. 407/841–8240). The cost is 75¢. The downtown area, however, is far from most hotels, so you might want to consider other options.

By Limousine **Airport Limousine Service of Orlando** (tel. 407/423–5566) sends 11-passenger vans to Disney World and along Rte. 192 every 30 minutes. Prices begin at $11 one way for adults, $6 for children 4–14; to $20 round-trip adults, $10 children 4–14. **Town & Country Limo** (tel. 407/828–3035) and **First Class Transportation** (tel. 407/351–5590) also offer limousine service between the airport and WDW. The trip takes about 35 minutes.

By Taxi Taxis are the fastest way to get from the airport to wherever you will be staying (25–30 minutes at most), but the ride won't be cheap. To Walt Disney World hotels or to hotels along U.S. 192 West, a cab trip will cost about $35 plus tip. To the International Drive area, it will cost about $25 plus tip. Cabs queue at the airport.

By Car When you leave the airport, catch the Beeline Expressway (Rte. 528) west to International Drive and exit at Sea World. Or stay on the Beeline to I–4, and head either west to Disney World or east to downtown Orlando. You would be wise to call your hotel for the best route.

By Car

If you want to have your car in Florida without having to drive it there, put it aboard the **Auto-Train** in Lorton, VA, near Washington, DC. The train goes to Sanford, FL, some 23 miles from Orlando.

By Train

Amtrak (tel. 800/USA–RAIL) stops in Winter Park (150 Morse Blvd.), in Orlando (1400 Sligh Blvd.), and then, 20 minutes later, in Kissimmee (416 Pleasant St.).

By Bus

Contact **Greyhound** (300 W. Amelia St., Orlando, tel. 407/843–7720) or consult your phone book or directory assistance for a local number that will automatically connect you with the national Greyhound Information Center.

Staying in Orlando

Important Addresses and Numbers

Tourist
Information

For **Walt Disney World** information and brochures, go to any ticket window or call 407/824–4321 daily 8 AM–9 PM.

The **Visitor Information Center** (8445 International Dr., in the Mercado Mediterranean Shopping Village, tel. 407/363–5800) is the main information office for the Orlando area.

Kissimmee–St. Cloud Tourist Information (1925 E. Irlo Bronson Memorial Hwy., tel. 407/847–5000) is 2½ miles east of I–4 on Rte. 192.

Emergencies **Police** or **Ambulance,** tel. 911.

Doctors   Hospital emergency rooms are open 24 hours a day. The most accessible hospital, located in the International Dr. area, is the **Orlando Regional Medical Center/Sand Lake Hospital** (9400 Turkey Lake Rd., tel. 407/351–8500).

For hotel-room visits by physicians for minor medical care and non-narcotic medicine, contact a mobile minor emergency service called **Housemed** (tel. 407/648–9234 and 407/846–2093 in Kissimmee).

For minor medical problems, visit the **Family Treatment Center** (6001 Vineland Rd., one block west of Kirkman Rd., tel. 407/351–6682). If you have no access to a car, the center will pick you up and bring you to its office.

24-Hour
Pharmacies

Eckerd Drugs (908 Lee Rd., Orlando, tel. 407/644–6908).

Walgreen Drug Store (2410 E. Colonial Dr., Orlando, tel. 407/894–6781).

Road Service   **AAA Emergency Road Service,** tel. 800/824–4432 or 407/896–1166.

24-Hour Market **Gooding's Supermarket** (7600 Dr. Phillips Blvd., tel. 407/352–8851) is conveniently located off I–4, a few blocks from International Drive.

Disney World   Walt Disney World Information, tel. 407/824–4321.

Accommodations Reservations, tel. 407/W–DISNEY.

Dinner Show Reservations, tel. 407/W–DISNEY.

WDW Resort Dining/Recreation Information, tel. 407/824–3737.

Tours (Magic Kingdom & Epcot Center), tel. 407/827–8233.

Magic Kingdom Lost & Found, tel. 407/824–4521.

Epcot Center Lost & Found, tel. 407/827–8236.

Car Care Center, tel. 407/824–4813.

Western Union at WDW, tel. 407/824–3456.

Banking Information (Sun Bank), tel. 407/824–5767.

Time and Weather, tel. 407/422–1611.

Walt Disney World Shopping Village Information, tel. 407/828–3058.

KinderCare Child Care, tel. 407/827–5444.

Getting Around

By Car The most important artery in the Orlando area is **Interstate 4 (I–4),** which many locals simply refer to as "the Expressway." This interstate ties everything together, and you'll invariably receive directions in reference to it. The problem is that I–4 is considered an east-west expressway in our national road system (the even numbers refer to an east-west orientation, the odd numbers to a north-south orientation). I–4 does run from east to west *if* you follow it from the Atlantic Coast to Florida's Gulf of Mexico. But in the Orlando area I–4 actually runs north and south. Always remember, therefore, that when the signs say east you are often going north, and when the signs say west, you are often going south. Think north-EAST and south-WEST.

Another main drag is **International Drive,** which has several major hotels, restaurants, and shopping centers. You can get onto International Drive from I–4 exits 28 and 29.

The other main road, **U.S. 192,** cuts across I–4 at exits 25A and 25B. This highway goes through the Kissimmee area and crosses Walt Disney World property, taking you to the Magic Kingdom's main entrance. U.S. 192 may sometimes be called by one of its former names, Spacecoast Parkway or Irlo Bronson Memorial Highway.

By Bus If you are staying along International Drive, in Kissimmee, or in Orlando proper, you can take advantage of the limited public bus system, but only to get places within the immediate area. To find out which bus to take, ask your hotel clerk or call the **Tri-County Transit Authority Information Office** (tel. 407/841–8240) during business hours. A transfer will add 10¢ to the regular 75¢ fare.

By Taxi Taxi fares start at $2.25 and cost $1.30 for each mile thereafter, with slightly higher rates during nighttime hours. Call **Yellow Cab Co.** (tel. 407/699–9999) or **Town and Country Cab** (tel. 407/828–3035).

From the Hotels to the Attractions There are many transportation services available, serving just about every hotel and major attraction in the area. Many offer both scheduled service and charters. All hotels can arrange pickups and drop-offs to and from attractions. Transportation usually costs less than $5 each way. For attractions such as Busch Gardens and Cypress Gardens, which are more than a half-hour's drive, expect to pay a single price of about $27 per person, which includes round-trip fare and admission. Different services schedule these trips on different days of the week. Call in advance for reservations. Companies offering both scheduled and charter transportation include **Gray Line of Or-**

Orlando Area

lando (tel. 407/422–0744), **Rabbit Bus Lines** (tel. 407/291–2424), and **Phoenix Tours** (tel. 407/859–7160).

Guided Tours

Walt Disney World   A good way of getting a feel for the layout of the Magic Kingdom, along with some interesting commentary about what goes on behind the scenes and inside tips on how to see the attractions in the most efficient way, is to take one of the guided orientation tours.

These 3½- to 4-hour tours cost $5 per adult and $3.50 per child, in addition to admission price. Tours include visits to some of the rides and pavilions, but don't expect to go to the head of the line. This is not like taking ski lessons; you still have to wait your turn even though you're with an official tour guide.

Departure times depend on demand. To find out the schedule, ask at the information desk in City Hall in the Magic Kingdom, or at Earth Station in Epcot Center, tel. 407/827–8233.

Boat Rides   **Rivership Romance.** Take a trip up the cypress-lined, densely forested St. John's River on a 110-foot, triple-decker catamaran for either a few hours or a couple of days. Trips include breakfasts, dinners, and weekend dinner dances with live music. The day trips take you through a peaceful, tropical landscape. You may see some interesting wildlife, such as manatees, blue herons, and bald eagles, but most of the time you'll be listening to the silence.

The *Romance* is a curious-looking modern boat with a sun deck, a lounge, and a dining room that serves some surprisingly good meals, with such dinner entrees as orange-glazed Cornish hen and crabmeat-stuffed whitefish. Visitors in search of nonstop fun may want to mutiny; others will relish this peaceful escape from the hectic pace of the mainland. The cost ranges from $17.14 to $36.19 per person ($190 for the overnight trip), including some meals. *Monroe Harbour, 433 N. Palmetto Ave., Sanford (from I–4 take Exit 51 and drive east 4 miles), tel. 800/423–7401 or 407/321–5091. Dress casual. Reservations required. MC, V.*

Helicopter Rides   **J.C. Helicopters.** Sign up for aerial tours of Disney World, Sea World, and other attractions. The flights at dark are spectacular. Prices start at $22.50 for adults, $10 for children. *Orlando Hyatt Heliport at I–4 and U.S. 192 (next to Disney World), tel. 407/847–7222.*
Falcon Helicopters. Tours of Orlando's attractions. Prices start at $29 for adults and $15 for children. *8990 International Dr., Orlando, tel. 407/352–1753.*

Ballooning   **Balloon Flights of Florida.** This Church Street Station event is not cheap, but it's an experience you'll never forget. The flight, flown by a balloonist who made the first trip across the Atlantic, is followed by brunch at Lili Marlene's. $140 per person. *129 W. Church St., Orlando, tel. 407/841–UPUP.*

Rise & Float Balloon Tours. Depart at dawn and indulge yourself in a champagne in-flight breakfast. *5767 Major Blvd., Orlando, tel. 407/352–8191.*

2 Portrait of Walt Disney

The Disney Version

by Richard Schickel

Mr. Schickel has reviewed movies for Time *since 1972. Before that he was film critic for* Life. *His many books include* The Disney Version *and* Intimate Strangers: The Culture of Celebrity.

Among unsophisticated people there was a common misapprehension that Disney continued to draw at least the important sequences in his animated films, his comic strips, his illustrated books. Although his studio often stressed in its publicity the numbers of people it employed and the beauties of their teamwork, some *very* unsophisticated people thought he did everything himself —an interesting example of the persistence of a particularly treasured illusion and of the corporation's ability to keep it alive even while denying it.

Disney himself once tried to explain his role in his company by telling a story that may well be apochryphal but is no less significant and no less quoted in company publicity for all that. "You know," he said, "I was stumped one day when a little boy asked, 'Do you draw Mickey Mouse?' I had to admit I did not draw any more. 'Then you think up all the jokes and ideas?' 'No,' I said, 'I don't do that.' Finally he looked at me and said, 'Mr. Disney, just what do you do?'

"'Well,' I said, 'sometimes I think of myself as a little bee. I go from one area of the studio to another and gather pollen and sort of stimulate everybody.' I guess that's the job I do."

The summary is not a bad one, as far as it goes. But there were a good many more wrinkles in Disney's situation than the smoothness of this explanation would indicate. For one thing, Disney was continually, if mildly, irked because he could not draw Mickey or Donald or Pluto. He never could. Even Mickey Mouse was designed by someone else, namely Ub Iwerks, an old friend from Disney's pre-Hollywood days. Iwerks actually received screen credit for so doing on the first Mouse cartoons. In later years Disney was known to apply to his animators for hints on how to render a quick sketch of Mickey in order to oblige autograph hunters who requested it to accompany his signature. Even more embarrassingly, he could not accurately duplicate the familiar "Walt Disney" signature that appeared as a trademark on all his products. There are people who received authentically autographed Disney books and records but who thought they were fake because his hand did not match that of the trademark—a particular irony in the case of Disney, who had devoted a lifetime to publicizing his name and, as we have seen, quite literally capitalizing on it.

Stories like these should not be taken to mean that Disney passed his final years living out the myth that money cannot

Reprinted from The Disney Version *(Touchstone, 1968) by permission of the author.*

buy happiness or that when his fortune caught up with his fame he found that all his dreams were a mockery. Far from it. Like many men who have grown rich through their own efforts, he had little use for personal display. His suits were still bought off the peg. His diet still consisted largely of the foods he had acquired a taste for in the hash houses of his youth (hamburgers, steaks and chops were staples; he especially liked chili). He drove himself to work, mostly in standard American cars, though in his last year he took to using the Jaguar that Roddy MacDowall had driven in *That Darned Cat*. He served tomato juice to visitors in his office but allowed beer to be served in the studio commissary—by no means a standard Hollywood practice—and admitted to enjoying a highball or two at the end of a workday that minimally ran twelve hours.

He traveled mainly on business and submitted to vacations with restless grouchiness. His one known extravagance was the scale model train that used to circle his home and that he conceived and then helped to build. In the early Fifties it had been his great pleasure to don a railroad engineer's cap, brandish a slender-spouted railroader's oilcan and pilot grandchildren and other visitors around his yard.

The train became, over the years, the subject of a disproportionate share of Disney lore. It was as if he used it to distract attention from other areas of his private life—certainly it made excellent feature copy for popular journalism. Mrs. Disney and his daughters tried to persuade him to build the thing at the studio instead of in his yard, but he went so far as to have his lawyers draft a right-of-way contract for his family to sign giving him permission to build and maintain the train. It was a token of such seriousness of intent that they agreed to sign it, whereupon he declared that in the circumstances their verbal consent was good enough for him. He loved fussing over the train, continually adding to its supply of rolling stock, improving the grades, even digging a tunnel so that it could pass under some of his wife's flower gardens without disturbing them. Mrs. Disney once commented, "It is a wonderful hobby for him . . . it has been a fine diversion and safety valve for his nervous energy. For when he leaves the studio he can't just lock the door and forget it. He is so keyed up he has to keep going on something."

She noted that a good deal of their social life in this period revolved around giving people rides on the half-mile line and that a select few were given cards designating them vice presidents of the road. She and her daughters quickly became bored with the train, but Disney did not, and he even suffered some hurt feelings over their indifference. He enjoyed—like a small boy with an electric train—planning wrecks because repairing the damage was so much fun. Once, after he bought two new engines, she heard him enthusing to George Murphy, the former Senator and then one of the toy train line's "vice presidents," "Boy, we're sure to have some wrecks now!"

The train was the only splash of color in the Disneys' quiet home life. Their friends, with the exception of Murphy, Kay Kayser, Irene Dunne and a few others, were not drawn from show business. Indeed, their daughter, Diane, became the first daughter of a motion-picture-industry family to make her debut at the Las Madrinas Ball in Los Angeles (which, in 1967, finally invited its first Jewish girl to participate). To old Angelenos the movies and the Jews were, apparently, virtually synonymous. Of the other aspects of Disney's mature home life little is known. He is recorded as having been a doting father, given to sentimental outbursts on such occasions as weddings and the birth of grandchildren, and the indulgent master of a poodle, for whom he was known to raid the ice box for cold meat. He also forbade the extermination of small pests—rabbits, squirrels and the like—that raided his wife's garden. This was, so far as one can tell, no idle image-protection on his part, but rather an expression of genuine concern for animal life. Outside the home his favorite recreation was wandering around— unrecognized, he hoped—in such places as the Farmer's Market in Los Angeles or on New York's Third Avenue, where he liked to browse the secondhand and antique shops and buy dollhouse-sized furniture. He had, Mrs. Disney reported, "no use for people who throw their weight around as celebrities, or for those who fawn over you just because you are famous."

Among countless perquisites that were available to him as the head of a prospering corporation, the only one that seemed to afford him much pleasure was the company's three-plane "airline," the flagship of which was a prop-jet Grumman Gulfstream. He went everywhere on it and took an open—perhaps even childlike— pride in this particular symbolization of his status. In the months before he died, he frequently mentioned the pure jet that Walt Disney Productions had on order and that, typically, was to be a model for the next generation of executive jets—a technological leader.

But the backyard train and the plane were in contrast with the essential Disney personality. The *Los Angeles Times*'s obituary editorial speculated that Disney's "real joy must have come from seeing the flash of delight sweep across a child's face and hearing his sudden laughter, at the first sight of Mickey Mouse, or Snow White or Pinocchio." Certainly the sight did not make him unhappy, but the *Times'* own biographical sketch, appearing in the same edition, carried a more nearly true statement from Disney himself on the source of his deepest satisfaction in his later years. A reporter once asked him, according to the piece, to name his most rewarding experience, and Disney's reply was blunt and brief: "The whole damn thing.

The fact that I was able to build an organization and hold it . . ."

These are clearly not the words of some kindly old uncle who just loves to come to your child's birthday party and do his magic tricks and tell his jokes and find his kicks in the kiddies' laughter and applause and their parents' gratitude. Neither do they appear to bear much resemblance to anything we might expect from an artist looking back over his career. They represent, instead, the entrepreneurial spirit triumphant. They are the words of a man who has struggled hard to establish himself and his product; who has fought his way in from the fringes of his chosen industry to its center; who has gambled his own money and his own future on his own innovative inspirations and organizational intelligence and more than once has come close to losing his whole bundle. They are, most of all, the words of a man who at last is in possession of the most important piece of information a player in the only really important American game can obtain—the knowledge that he is a sure economic winner, that no matter what happens the chance of his being busted out of the game has been eliminated and that his accumulated winnings will surely survive him.

This knowledge was vouchsafed by Disney only late in life, but when it was, he was fond of working variations on the theme that money was merely a fertilizer, useful only to the degree that it could make new crops of ideas and enterprises grow. This is, of course, an image that anyone brought up in the spirit of the Protestant ethic would instantly appreciate and probably applaud; it is also an image that Freud, and more particularly his latter-day followers into the dark realms where the relationship between money and feces are explored, would quickly—probably too quickly—understand and explicate at dismal length. To a builder of Disney's character, though, money did in fact perform precisely the function he liked to describe, and its symbolic value was in good part just what it seemed most obviously to be—a measure of distances traveled, a way of keeping score.

Looking back, it is easy to see that Disney was neither a sold-out nor a sidetracked artist. He was a man who had obtained what he truly wanted: elevation—at least on the lower levels—to the ranks of the other great inventor-entrepreneurs of our industrial history. He was of the stuff of Ford and Edison, a man who could do everything a great entrepreneur is expected to do—dream and create and hold.

To see Disney as merely the proprietor of a mouse factory is to miss entirely his significance as a primary force in the expression and formation of the American mass consciousness. One must, at last, take him seriously, because whatever the literary content of his works, however immature his conscious vision of his own motives and achievements was, there was undeniably some almost mystic bond between himself and the moods and styles and attitudes of this people. He could not help but reflect and summarize these things in his almost every action. We have been taught to understand that the medium is the message, and it seems indubitable that there was a message in each of the media that Disney conquered, a message that transcended whatever he thought—or we thought—he was saying. When we seemed to demand an optimistic myth he gave us the unconquerable Mouse. When we seemed to demand the sense of continuity implicit in reminders of our past, he gave us fairy tales in a form we could easily accept. When we demanded neutral, objective factuality, he gave us the nature films. When, in a time of deep inner stress, we demanded another kind of unifying vision, he gave us a simplified and rosy-hued version of the small town and rural America that may have formed our institutions and our heritage but no longer forms us as individuals. When we demanded, at last, not formal statements but simply environments in which to lose ourselves, he gave us those in the amusement parks.

His statements were often vulgar. They were often tasteless, and they often exalted the merely technological over the sensitively humane. They were often crassly commercial, sickeningly sentimental, crudely comic. But the flaws in the Disney version of the American vision were hardly unique to him. They are flaws that have crept into it over decades, and they are the flaws almost universally shared by the nation's citizens.

Balanced against them must be the virtues he shared with his countrymen as well—his individualism, his pragmatism, his will to survive, his appreciation of the possibilities inherent in technological progress, despite the bad odor it often gives off today. Above all, there was the ability to build and build and build—never stopping, never looking back, never finishing—the institution that bears his name. There is creativity of a kind in this, and it is a creativity that is not necessarily of a lesser order than artistic creativity. "The American mechanizes as freely as an old Greek sculpted, as the Venetian painted," a 19th-century English observer of our life once said, and it is sheer attitudinizing not to see in our mechanized institutions one of the highest expressions of this peculiar genius of ours. These industrial institutions may ultimately be our undoing, but it is being blind to history not to see that they were our making as well. It is culturally blind not to see that Disney was a forceful and, in his special way, imaginative worker in this, our only great tradition. The only fitting honor to be paid him is to associate him firmly with it and not with some artistic tradition that was fundamentally alien to him and invoked standards inappropriate to the evaluation of of his accomplishments. The industrial and entrepreneurial tradition that both moved and sheltered him was neither more nor less flawed than he was.

And so there is a certain appropriateness about his last works. Film is, after all, a transitory thing, as all works of art are in comparison to that thing that every American knows to abide—the land. Or as we prefer to think of it, real estate. At heart, Disneyland is the very stuff of the American Dream—improved land, land with buildings and machinery on it, land that is increasing in value day by day, thanks to its shrewd development. With its success Disney realized the dream that had been denied his father and that had driven Disney as it drives so many of us. The day before he died, he lay in his hospital bed, staring at the ceiling, envisioning the squares of acoustical tile as a grid map of Disneyworld in Florida, saying things like, "This is where we'll put the monorail. And we'll run the highway right here." Truly, he had found The Magic Kingdom.

Typically, this was a secret he kept to himself. To be sure, he told anyone who bothered to inquire that he was not a producer of children's entertainment, that in fact he had never made a film or a television show or an exhibit at Disneyland that did not have, as its primary criterion of success, its ability to please him. And he often admitted that his great pleasure was the *business* he had built, not the products it created. But he—and most especially his organization—did nothing to discourage the misunderstanding of his work and his motives. And so much did we want to believe that he was a kind of Pied Piper whose principal delight was speaking, for altruistic and sentimental reasons, the allegedly universal language of childhood, so much did we *need* an essentially false picture of him, that the public clung to this myth almost as tightly as an eager Wall Street hugged to its gray flannel bosom the delightful reports on the recent economic performance of Walt Disney Productions. The commercial statistics were powerful enough to send the price of the stock to the highest levels in history *after* Disney died, even though the only foreboding its analysts expressed about it in the 1960s was based precisely on the fear of the founder's death and the inability of his executives to carry on in the great tradition. The myth of the Disney personality became similarly inflated after his passing. It was well expressed by the correspondent of *Paris Match* who, in an obituary cover story (Mickey was displayed in full color, crying), reached an unprecedented—and quite possibly fictive—mawkishness, with his description of the scene at the hospital on the day of Disney's death:

"At St. Joseph's Christmas party, the delighted children were applauding the trained dog act and singing 'Oh, Tannenbaum.'

"The hospital chaplain stepped out of the room where the successful life of Walt Disney had just come to an end.

"'Lying there, he looks like Gulliver with his dream menagerie gathered around him,' he whispered."

One likes to think that, however pleased Disney might have been by the sentiment, there was a secret recess of his mind where he kept a rather precise accounting of who he was and what he was. Ray Bradbury, the writer, once conceived the notion of having Disney run for mayor of Los Angeles on the not completely unreasonable ground that he was the only man with enough technological imagination to rationalize the sprawling mess the megapolis had become. He journeyed out to the studio to put the idea to Disney, who was flattered but declined the opportunity. "Ray," he asked, "why should I run for mayor when I'm already king?"

And so he even managed to speak his own best epitaph, the one he always feared someone would speak for him. Like all his other works it seemed fanciful only at first glance. At heart, it was completely realistic.

3 Exploring Walt Disney World

Getting There

Walt Disney World has its own complete transportation system to get you wherever you want to go. Yet because the property is so extensive—27,400 acres, 98 of them for the Magic Kingdom and another 260 for Epcot—the system can be a bit confusing, even for an experienced Disney visitor.

Best known is the elevated monorail that connects Disney World's biggest resorts and attractions. There are also extensive bus, motor launch, and ferry systems.

If you are staying at an on-site resort or a Walt Disney World Village hotel, or if you hold a combination Magic Kingdom–Epcot Center ticket, on-site transportation is free. If not, you can buy yourself unlimited transportation within Disney World for $2.50 a day.

By Car If you arrive at either the Magic Kingdom or Epcot Center by car, there is a $3 parking charge. If you're staying at a Disney World hotel, show your guest ID for free parking.

Make sure to remember or write down exactly where you park; you'll have an awfully long wait before the sea of automobiles has departed and yours is the only one left. Trams make frequent trips between the parking areas and the park's turnstiles.

If your car won't start or it breaks down in Disney World, the **Car Care Center** near the Toll Plaza to the Magic Kingdom offers emergency road service. Open weekdays 7 AM–6 PM, tel. 407/824–4813.

By Motor Launch These boats depart about every 20 minutes, and use color-coded flags to identify their route. They are for the use of resort guests only, with the exception of day guests with special activity tickets (i.e., to Discovery Island or River Country).

Blue—Connects the Contemporary Resort with the Fort Wilderness Resort Area and Discovery Island every 15 minutes between 10 AM and 10 PM.

Gold—Connects the Grand Floridian, Magic Kingdom, and Polynesian Resort at 15- to 25-minute intervals from 30 minutes before the Magic Kingdom opens until it closes, with pickup only from the Magic Kingdom until the park clears.

Green—Connects the Magic Kingdom, Fort Wilderness Resort Area, and Discovery Island (when it is open) every 20–25 minutes from half an hour before opening until closing time.

By Ferry A ferry service runs across Seven Seas Lagoon connecting the Transportation and Ticket Center (TTC) with the Magic Kingdom. The huge gleaming white crafts depart from each side of the lagoon about every 12 minutes when the Magic Kingdom is open. They can at times get you to the Magic Kingdom faster than the monorail. It is a comfortable ride, gliding over the lagoon's silky waters. Most people heading for the Magic Kingdom opt for the monorail and then take the ferry back at day's end for a chance to relax. If you want to avoid the worst of the lines for both monorail and ferry, take the opposite tack.

By Monorail This elevated train of the future operates daily from 7:30 AM to 11 PM (or until one hour after the Magic Kingdom closes). The monorail does not go everywhere. It is a fun way to travel, and the air-conditioning is a godsend on a sweltering day; but be prepared for delays during busy periods because of mechanical problems or overcrowding.

The central connecting station for the monorail is called the **Transportation and Ticket Center** (TTC). One monorail line goes from the TTC to the Magic Kingdom and back in a loop around Seven Seas Lagoon. This is primarily for visitors who are not guests at the on-site resorts. Another line connects the TTC with the Contemporary Resort, the Magic Kingdom, the Grand Floridian, and the Polynesian. A third line goes directly from the TTC to Epcot. The TTC is where you can transfer between the Disney bus system and the monorail.

When you get to a monorail station ask an attendant if you can sit up in the conductor's cabin, called "the nose" by the crew. If there is room, the ride up front is much more exciting than sitting back in one of the regular cabins. It makes the kids feel important, and even adults will get a kick out of it.

By Bus The bus system seems more complicated than it is. Each bus carries a small color-coded and/or letter-coded pennant on the front and sides. Here's where they take you:

Green—Connects Disney Inn and Polynesian Village Resort with the TTC. This line operates every 15 minutes from 7 AM to 2 AM.

Blue—Connects Fort Wilderness Resort Area with the TTC. These buses operate every 8 minutes from 7 AM to 2 AM.

Green-and-Gold—If the pennant has the letters EC/V on it, the bus connects Epcot, the Resort Villas, Disney Village Clubhouse, and Disney Village Marketplace. If the bus has the letters MK on it, it travels only between the TTC and the villas. These lines operate every 20 minutes from 7 AM to 2 AM.

Silver-and-Red Stripe—Connects Walt Disney World Village Hotel Plaza and Epcot Center. This bus operates every 20 minutes from 8 AM until two hours after Epcot closes.

Red and White—Connects Walt Disney World Village Hotel Plaza and the TTC. This line operates every 20 minutes, from 8 AM to until about two hours after the Magic Kingdom closes.

Red—Connects TTC and Disney Village Marketplace with Epcot. This line operates at 15- to 25-minute intervals from 8 AM to 2 AM.

Gold—Connects the Grand Floridian, Polynesian Resort and Contemporary Resort with the TTC at 15- to 25-minute intervals from 7 AM to 2AM.

Orange-and-White Stripe—If the pennant has the letters MK on it, the bus connects Caribbean Beach Resort with the TTC from 7 AM until 2 AM. If the bus has the letters EC on it, it connects Epcot and Caribbean Beach Resort from 8 AM to two hours after Epcot closes. Both lines run at 15- to 25-minute intervals.

Brown—A Fort Wilderness Transportation Circle line. It connects the Trading Post, Trail Blaze Corral, the Outpost, Loops 600-1300, Loops 2100-2800, and the Meadow Recreation Complex from 7 AM to 2 AM at 15- to 25-minute intervals.

Walt Disney World

Lake Reams

Lake Tibet

Lake Mabel

Lake Sheen

Reams Rd.

Cast Dr.

N

535

The Magic Kingdom

Bay Lake

South Lake

Winter Garden - Vineland Rd.

Discovery Island

Bay Lake

Zoological Park

River Country

West Wilderness Rd.

Fort Wilderness Campground

Bonnet Creek

535

Monorail

Floridian Way

World Dr.

Monorail

Vista Blvd.

Fort Wilderness Tr.

Vista Blvd.

Bonnett Creek Rd.

Buena Vista Dr.

Cypress Creek

Main Entrance

Reedy Creek

Main Entrance

Epcot Center Dr.

Community Dr.

Epcot Center

World Dr.

Buena Vista Dr.

Reedy Creek

Epcot Center Dr.

EXIT 26

World Dr.

4

0   1 mile
0   1 km

192

EXIT 25

Silver—Another Fort Wilderness Transportation Circle line. It connects Creekside Meadow Group Camping with Loops 300-500 and Loops 1400-2300 from 7 AM to 2 AM at 15- to 25-minute intervals.

Orange—The Caribbean Beach Resort internal transportation line, operates from 7 AM to 2 AM about every 20 minutes.

Admission

Visiting Walt Disney World is not cheap, especially if you have a child or two along. There are no discounted family tickets.

Seven different types of admission tickets are sold in one of two categories—adult, meaning everyone 10 and older, and children 3–9.

The word "ticket" is used by Disney World to mean only a single day's admission to either the Magic Kingdom or Epcot Center. The price is $28 for adults and $22 for children. If you want to spend two days visiting either one or both attractions, you have to buy a separate ticket each day. For more than two days, Disney World offers what it calls the Passport, which admits you to both the Magic Kingdom and Epcot Center, along with unlimited use of the internal transportation system.

Here is a list of prices. They are subject to change, so call for confirmation.

One-day ticket	$29 adults, $23 children
Four-day passport	$97 adults, $77 children; *$94/$75**
Five-day passport	$112 adults, $90 children; *$107/$85**
River Country, one day	$11.75 adults, $9.25 children; *$10.75/$8.25**
River Country, two days	$17.75 adults, $13.75 children; *$16.75/$12.75**
Discovery Island, one day	$7.50 adults, $4 children
Combined River Country/Discovery Island, one day	$15 adults, $11 children; *$14/$10**
Annual pass	$180 adults, $155 children

*visitors staying in a Disney World Resort or in a resort in the WDW Village Hotel Plaza

Passports are available for four or five days. They can save you a great deal of money, and may be advisable even if you're staying in the area for only two days. Each time you use a passport the entry date is stamped on it; remaining days may be used any time in the future. If you buy a one-day ticket and later decide to extend your visit, you can get full credit for it toward the purchase of any passport. Exchanges can be made at City Hall in the Magic Kingdom or at Earth Station in Epcot. Do this before leaving the park; once you've left, the ticket is worthless.

Tickets and passports to Disney World and Epcot can be pur-chased at admission booths at the TTC, in all on-site resorts (if you're a registered guest), or at the Walt Disney World kiosk on the second floor of the main terminal at Orlando International Airport. If you want to buy them before arriving in Orlando, send a check or money order to Admissions, Walt Disney World, Box 10000, Lake Buena Vista, FL 32830. Remember, it usually takes four to six weeks for the order to be processed, so write well in advance.

If you want to leave the Magic Kingdom or Epcot Center and return on the same day, be sure to have your hand stamped on the way out. You'll need your ticket *and* the hand-stamp to be readmitted.

Operating Hours

Operating hours for the Magic Kingdom and Epcot vary widely throughout the year and change for school and legal holidays. In general, the longest days are during the prime summer months and when the Magic Kingdom is open to midnight and Epcot is open to 11 PM.

At other times of the year, Epcot is open until 8 PM and the Magic Kingdom is open to 6 PM, with Main Street remaining open until 7.

It's important to remember that though the Magic Kingdom and Epcot officially open at 9 AM, visitors may enter at 8:30, and sometimes at 8. Arriving before the official opening time, you can enjoy breakfast in the Magic Kingdom, make dinner reservations before the crowds arrive, and be among the first on line for the most popular attractions when they open at 9.

Ratings

Specific attractions in the Magic Kingdom and Epcot Center have been rated according to general audience response to the quality of the ride or show, in comparison to other attractions within Disney World. Ratings do not indicate the size of the crowd that will be encountered at the particular attractions, but rather suggest how enjoyable visitors seem to regard the attractions. The following ratings were determined by sam-pling visitors' opinions as they departed the attractions:

Very popular (most enjoyable)
Popular
Moderately popular
Not very popular
Unpopular (least enjoyable)

At Epcot's World Showcase, the national pavilions are enjoy-able for audiences of all ages; however, young children may consider this cultural fare less exciting than the fantasy-oriented attractions at the Magic Kingdom, and they may find all the walking required an exhausting experience.

Magic Kingdom

When people think of Disney World, it is the Magic Kingdom that sparks their imaginations. This is the main event in Orlando, the center-ring attraction that draws millions of people to central Florida year after year. Mickey arm-in-arm with a joyful young guest beneath Cinderella's fairytale castle; jungle cruises and space mountains; cartoon characters dancing through a fantasyland as a high-pitched chorus sings refrains from "It's a Small World"—these are images that have burned their way into our national consciousness. The Magic Kingdom offers 45 major attractions in six different "lands" spread across 98 acres. Many of the rides are geared for the young but most of them can be enjoyed by the young at heart. Even those who dread amusement parks can't help but be awed by the scope of Disney's vision.

Getting There

By car, take I–4 west to the clearly marked exit sign for the Magic Kingdom. This will put you on U.S. 192 west. It's a four-mile drive along Disney's main entrance road to the toll gate, and another mile to the huge parking area. Each of the 12 areas is named for a Disney cartoon character (Donald, Pluto, etc.) and every parking space has its own number. Tractor-drawn trams pass frequently through the parking areas and whisk you to the monorail and ferry, which will take you to the gates of the Kingdom.

If you're staying at the Contemporary, Polynesian Village, or Grand Floridian resorts, just hop aboard the monorail. From the Disney Inn, take a Green bus; from the Fort Wilderness Resort Area, you'll need either a Blue bus or a Green motor launch. From the Resort Villas, take a bus with a green-and-gold pennant and an MK designation.

It's an arduous journey, just getting to the gates of the Magic Kingdom (during summer or other busy seasons, be prepared for serious bumper-to-bumper traffic both on I–4 nearing the U.S. 192 exit and on 192 itself), but this is the way Walt Disney wanted it. When Disneyland opened in California, the lush orange groves that surrounded the park soon turned into an ugly mass of commercial development. Disney did not want this to happen at the Orlando site, so he surrounded his Magic Kingdom with a broad buffer zone of forests and fields. Disney also wanted to create in visitors the effect of leaving their work-a-day lives behind.

Orientation

Numbers in the margin correspond with points of interest on the Magic Kingdom map.

The first plaza you enter is Town Square. City Hall is on your left, MGM studios are on your right, and the Railroad Station is directly behind you. Stretching before you is Main Street—a boulevard filled with Victorian-style stores and dining spots. Walk two blocks along Main Street, and you will enter Central Plaza with Cinderella's Castle rising up directly in front of you. This is the hub of the Kingdom; all of the "lands" radiate out from it, like wedges of a pie. Town Square is the starting point of the daily parade (usually 3–3:20 PM) of cartoon characters.

On your immediate left as you stand in the center of Central Plaza is a bridge leading to Adventureland, where you will find the Jungle Cruise, Pirates of the Caribbean, and a few other attractions. To your left, and a bit ahead, is a bridge leading to Frontierland and Liberty Square. These two smaller lands offer Big Thunder Mountain Railroad, Haunted Mansion, boat rides, and other shows. Adventureland, Frontierland, and Liberty Square are the lands with the greatest appeal for adults.

❶ Directly in front of you, as you stand in Central Plaza, is a passageway through the **Cinderella Castle** to Fantasyland. All the rides here are primarily for children, with the exception of 20,000 Leagues Under the Sea, which is recommended for visitors of all ages.

To the right of the Cinderella Castle is a path that takes you to the border between Fantasyland and Tomorrowland. Cross the bridge on your immediate right and you're in Tomorrowland, with little of interest to most visitors except for the dizzying Space Mountain ride.

Paths take you from one neighboring land to the next; however, if you want to get to a land that is "two or more wedges of the pie away," it may be faster to go back through Central Plaza. You can also take advantage of the Swiss-made Skyway gondola that connects the Liberty Square side of Fantasyland to Tomorrowland. The Skyway offers a bird's-eye view of these two lands, but it is not exactly rapid transportation.

It's not as long a walk from one land to the next as you might think, but don't think you can do the whole Kingdom in a day. Even if the crowds are small, see what interests you most and plan to return later. Remember, the early morning and late evening are the times when you can see and do the most.

Town Square

❷ **City Hall.** First stop in Town Square should be City Hall, which will be on your left, next to Sun Bank. City Hall has an information desk where you can pick up the *Magic Kingdom Guide Book* and a schedule of daily events (you should save time by getting a copy in advance at a Disney hotel or writing for one before you leave home). City Hall has a lost-and-found both for property and for people. Should anyone in your party get lost or separated, this is where to go. Nearby, beneath the Railroad, are coin deposit lockers where bags, stuffed animals, and so on can be stored.

❸ **WDW Railroad.** A great way to get an overview of the Kingdom is to hop aboard the Railroad and take a 14-minute, 1.5-mile ride around the entire perimeter of the park. You can board at the Victorian-style station that you pass beneath to enter Town Square. Until recently, the only other station was in Frontierland. A new station has been built to provide access to Mickey's Birthdayland on the border between Tomorrowland and Fantasyland.

The train is pulled by a steam engine that was built in Philadelphia in 1916. It was brought to Disney World from the Yucatán peninsula of Mexico, where early in the century it was used to transport sugarcane.

Main Street

The atmosphere is Hollywood Victorian in this Disney version of small-town America. Behind the facades are clothing and gift shops circa 1990. At least four points of interest are more than skin-deep.

The Walt Disney Story. On the right (east) side of Town Square, opposite City Hall, is a yellow Victorian house where a film and some Disney memorabilia offer insights into Disney's life and the empire he created.

Main Street Vehicles. A little red fire engine, a horseless carriage, a jitney, an omnibus, even a horse-drawn trolley—these are among the vehicles you can ride along the street.

Main Street Cinema. On your right as you leave Town Square and walk toward Cinderella's Castle is a silent-movie house that shows several films simultaneously on five screens—everything from Disney's earliest Mickey Mouse cartoons to slapstick, Keystone Kops–type flicks. This is entertaining for adults, and seldom too crowded.

Penny Arcade. Midway down Main Street, on the left, is a large game room with everything from moving-picture boxes and player pianos to the newest high-tech electronic video games. Quarters will be consumed here as fast as you can put them into your children's hands. Adults can spend a small fortune, too, on the old-fashioned Kiss-O-Meters.

Adventureland

These soft adventures to far-off lands are among the most crowded in the Kingdom. Visit first thing in the morning or as late in the afternoon as possible, or, better yet, in the evening.

Swiss Family Robinson Treehouse. *Popular; all ages.* The first attraction you will see is an outdoor, walk-through exhibit showing how the Swiss Family Robinson might have lived on their tropical island. Visitors walk up stairs and ramps into a realistic-looking tree made of cement and metal. It can take five minutes or as long as 25 minutes to pass through in single file. If there is a line, you may want to leave the family on their island, move on to the Jungle Cruise, and come back, say, after dinner.

❹ **Jungle Cruise.** *Very popular; all ages.* Canopied explorer launches take visitors on a journey along the Nile, through an Amazon rain forest, across an African jungle, and so on. Along the way you pass through a world of angry hippopotami, roaring lions, hungry cannibals, and bathing elephants that spray your boat. Good thing you have a tour guide to protect you through these treacherous waters and humor you with stories of less fortunate passengers who never made it through the journey. Kids eat it up, and everyone is amused. The ride itself takes only 10 minutes, but the line can take as long as an hour. Go as soon as the park opens, during the parade time (3–3:20 PM), or after 5 PM. Avoid 10 AM to noon.

❺ **Pirates of the Caribbean.** *Very popular; all ages.* Journey through a world of pirate strongholds and treasure-filled dungeons as G-rated seafarers swig their booze, sing chanteys, and revel in their booty and their women. The special effects, com-

The Magic Kingdom

Cinderella Castle, **1**
City Hall, **2**
WDW Railroad, **3**
Jungle Cruise, **4**
Pirates of the Caribbean, **5**
Big Thunder Mt. RR, **6**
Country Bear, **7**
Tom Sawyer Island, **8**
Fort Sam Clemens, **9**
Haunted Mansion, **10**
Hall of Presidents, **11**
20,000 Leagues, **12**
It's a Small World, **13**
Space Mountain, **14**
American Journeys, **15**
Grand Prix, **16**
Mickey's House, **17**
Mickey's Hollywood Theatre, **18**
Grandma Duck's Farm, **19**

FRONTIERLAND

Railroad Station

ADVENTURELAND

FANTASYLAND

MICKEY'S
BIRTHDAYLAND

Railroad
Station

17

18

19

13

12

Skyway to
Tomorrowland

Columbia
Harbour
House

1

11

16

14

LIBERTY
SQUARE

TOMORROWLAND

Skyway to
Fantasyland

15

WEDway
People Mover

Crystal
Palace

Carousel of
Progress

First Aid
Station

MAIN STREET
U.S.A.

2

3

Monorail
to Epcot

Ferry Landing

plete with Audio-Animatronics pirates and animals, are first class. Lines fluctuate throughout the day, but move fairly quickly. Best time is 2–3:30 PM and after 5 PM. Avoid 10 AM to noon.

Tropical Serenade—Enchanted Tikki Birds. *Not very popular, but still crowded; for children.* These were the first Audio-Animatronics creations, and it shows. The ceiling is covered with hundreds of exotic birds that jest and sing, but it is difficult to tell which bird is talking at any given time and even children find the show a bit confusing and not one of the park's top attractions. The tropical backdrop is worth a look—but you have to see the show to do so.

Frontierland

"Frontier Fun" is the theme of this gold-rush town of the Southwest.

6 **Big Thunder Mountain Railroad.** *Very popular; children must be at least 4'2".* As rollercoasters go, the ride is tame. But it's fun and exciting, nonetheless, to pitch and swerve around hills and into valleys, through a coal mine, a gold digger's settlement, and a ghost town. It's a fast, fun ride that is sure to get your heart pounding. It's also one of only two fast rides in the park (the other is Space Mountain). Try to go in the evening when the mountain is all lit up and lines are relatively short. Don't confuse this ride with the Walt Disney World Railroad that has a station in Frontierland.

7 **Country Bear Vacation Hoedown.** *Moderately popular; all ages.* This is an unabashedly corny stage show in which furry Audio-Animatronics bears joke, sing, and play down-home, country music and 1950s rock 'n' roll. It is a show for children or for anyone who loves puns.

Diamond Horseshoe Jamboree. *Popular; all ages.* An Old-Western saloon is the setting for this live stage show featuring all sorts of singing, dancing, and innocently rowdy entertainment. Sandwiches and light refreshments may be purchased before curtain time. You must make reservations early in the morning at the Hospitality House on Main Street because there are only five shows a day. Reservations are handed out on a first-come, first-served basis, with the strongest demand usually for the noon and 1:30 PM shows. Other shows are at 3, 4:30, and 6 PM.

8 **Tom Sawyer Island.** *Not very popular; all ages.* A raft takes you across the Rivers of America to an island where walking paths **9** lead to a cave, a couple of bouncy bridges, and **Fort Sam Clemens.** There is not much to see, but a sojourn here is a pleasant respite from the crowded mainland.

Liberty Square

This small land adjoins and blends into Frontierland. Its theme is Colonial History, and it consists of Early American-style shops and eating places. It has a few decent but tame attractions. Don't miss the chocolate chip cookies at the Snackspot next to Heritage House.

10 **Haunted Mansion.** *Very popular; all ages.* Ghosts and goblins haunt you at every turn through this eerie world of attics, dungeons, and graveyards. The special effects can seem very realistic and the buggies you ride in swivel from side to side. This attraction is not exactly frightening, but young children might disagree. It is one of the most imaginative attractions in the park. The best time to go is in the early morning or evening. Avoid noon–4 PM.

Liberty Square Riverboats. *Moderately popular; all ages.* This is a low-key attraction that takes you on an authentic-looking paddlewheel steamboat for a half-mile cruise through the "Rivers of America," passing along the way a series of reenacted scenes from the Wild West. It's not great entertainment, but it can be a comfortable escape from the crowds and the sun.

⑪ Hall of Presidents. *Moderately popular; adults or mature children.* When it first opened, this theatrical portrait of Presidents past and present caused quite a sensation because it was here that the first refinements of the Audio-Animatronics system could be seen in action. Although the show may now seem a bit slow and unexciting, it is interesting to hear the Disney view of American history and watch the seemingly immobile Presidents suddenly stand. Young children may find it boring, and if you have seen American Adventure at Epcot, you may, too. However, you may enjoy brushing up on a few major episodes in our nation's history, and the figures are strikingly realistic. Arrive several minutes before the show begins so you can take a look at the many historical artifacts on display in the rotunda, such as Revolutionary-era flags, muskets, and portraits.

Fantasyland

This is a land in which storybook dreams come true, and young children are very much in their element. The rides are all quite mild. There are a few traditional amusement park rides with Disney themes, such as the **Mad Tea Party,** where teacups spin around a big tea pot. Other favorites are **Dumbo the Flying Elephant** and a spectacular merry-go-round. There are several other indoor rides that spook and enchant children as they pass through a cartoon world filled with many familiar fairytale characters. Fantasyland is not exclusively for children, though; several attractions will interest adults as well.

⑫ 20,000 Leagues Under the Sea. *Very popular; all ages.* Inspired by the Jules Verne novel, this is one of the most popular attractions in the park, and one of the most elaborate. The notorious Captain Nemo takes you in his tightly packed Nautilus submarine to explore a beautiful and dangerous undersea world full of curious aquatic creatures. As the submarine circles the lagoon and penetrates a treacherous cavern, passengers gaze out through submerged portholes at lifelike vegetation, fish, tortoises, divers, and even a giant killer squid. Looking out through the portholes, you really do feel as though you are penetrating the ocean depths. There isn't much action in these waters, but it is quite a spectacle, and quite a vessel. Lines move very slowly, so go the first thing in the morning or late in the evening.

Magic Journeys. *Popular; all ages.* Put on a pair of 3-D glasses and have fun with the illusion of being bombarded by images that seem to fly at you from off the movie screen. After standing in a small, cramped room to watch a brief Disney 3-D cartoon from the 1930s, visitors move into another theater where they sit to watch the main event—a rather ingenuous film made for Epcot Center's Imagination Pavilion about some children's fantasy of joining a circus. The premise is fatuous, but sweet, and children enjoy it.

Mr. Toad's Wild Ride, Snow White's Adventures, Peter Pan's Flight. *Popular; for younger children.* These are all very similar types of indoor rides that take children on fairytale adventures. Both Mr. Toad and Snow White have many startling noises and scary images that may frighten very young children. Peter Pan's Flight is a great ride in the sky for children of all ages. The flight to Never-Never Land over moonlit London is spectacular, and so are many of the other special effects created with black light, fluorescent paint, and a lot of imagination.

⑬ It's a Small World. *Very popular; young children.* In this famous attraction originally created for New York's 1964–65 World's Fair, gaily dancing and singing puppets garbed in colorful native dress from many nations convey the timeless hope for peace and harmony in the world. The background music is sing-song but unforgettable, and the idea is positively saccharine. But kids love it nonetheless.

Tomorrowland

"Fun in the Future" is the motto of this section. Save it for the future if your time is limited; except for Space Mountain, all the rides are pretty unspectacular. The major problem is that what in 1970 was a look into the future now often seems rather dated. Another problem is that most of the attractions are sponsored by large corporations, and the audience is bombarded by commercial advertising at every turn. Visitors who want this sort of entertainment can get it at home, sitting on their living-room couches; or they can see better versions of it over at Epcot.

Despite its limitations, however, Tomorrowland has some redeeming traits. A few of the rides are fun for young children, and Space Mountain is an exciting ride for anybody who has the stomach for it. Also, the lines in this land are among the shortest.

⑭ Space Mountain. *Very popular; children must be at least 3; children under 7 must be accompanied by an adult.* This space-age, cone-shaped building is a landmark in the Kingdom. The roller coaster may never get to speeds over 20 miles per hour, but the experience in the dark, with everyone screaming and "stars" and "meteors" all around, is thrilling, even for hard-core roller coaster fans. Don't take any loose objects on the ride with you, because your hands will be too busy holding on and objects can easily fall out of cars as they dip and turn. You may even want to hold on to your children's wallets while they ride. To see the interior without taking the ride, hop aboard the People Mover.

⑮ American Journeys, CircleVision, Carousel of Progress, Mission to Mars. *Unpopular; all ages.* Each attraction lasts some 20 minutes and for some of you it will be 20 minutes too long. *Mission to Mars* is a theatrical, two-part, standing-and-sitting journey to Mars, taking you from the emission control room to your blast-off chamber where you watch some rather tired 7th-grade vintage film footage of outer space. *Carousel of Progress* is a theater that revolves around a series of stages with Audio-Animatronics characters that depict the evolution of technology in the American home through the 20th century. *American Journeys*, a film in CircleVision with nine movie screens, takes a patriotic look at the landscape of America. The quality is below that of CircleVision at Epcot.

Dream Flight. *Popular; all ages.* This attraction takes you on a ride through the history of aviation. It's the newest attraction, sponsored by Delta, which replaced *If You Could Fly.*

Starjets. *Moderately popular; for children.* These are small planes that circle around a rocket tower, rising and dipping as they go. Pleasant, but not worth waiting in a long line to experience.

⑯ Grand Prix Raceway. *Popular; children must be at least seven to go alone.* Mini race cars sputter along a winding tract at breathtaking speeds of up to seven miles per hour. The cars are guided along rails but have their own steering and brakes. Children who do not meet age and height requirements must be accompanied by adults.

Mickey's Birthdayland

Built to celebrate Mickey Mouse's 60th birthday in 1988, the newest of the Magic Kingdom's lands is a big hit with children. Guests catch the railroad at Main Street or Frontierland and take it to Duckburg, where they can view some of Mickey's famous cartoons and films, visit Mickey's house, meet Mickey for some photos, and join in Mickey's surprise birthday party, which has even the adults laughing when they leave. For parents who want to rest their feet, there is a playground, a petting zoo, and a maze for the children.

⑰ Mickey's House. *Popular; for younger children.* Stroll through the house and enjoy the memorabilia. When you walk out the back door, you are in the birthday party tent, where you catch some old film clips, help Minnie in the kitchen, and enjoy the surprise party thrown for Mickey by his buddies. The children will love it.

⑱ Mickey's Hollywood Theatre. *Very popular; for younger children.* Here is a chance to have your children pose with Mickey in an orderly one-on-one opportunity, rather than trying to fight the crowds throughout the park when Mickey is spotted strolling around.

⑲ Grandma Duck's Farm. *Moderately popular; for children.* You will never again see a farmyard so clean, but there are real barnyard babies to pet.

Time Out Visitors who care about real food will discover that gourmet dining is as much a fantasy as everything else in the Magic Kingdom. Fast food is king, and even the few sit-down, full-service restaurants are more like themed coffee shops than serious places to dine. What you will find are plenty of snack stands with hamburgers, hot dogs, pizza, pastries, cookies, and burritos. Visitors may want to create their own picnic lunches from a deli outside the Kingdom, store it in one of the lockers beneath the Railroad Station in Town Square, and eat it on a park bench or at a table in a fast-food joint. If you want to sit down to a meal, there are a few places to go. Lunch entrees range from $5 to $10, and dinner entrees range from $15 to $20. If you have just a day to spend and are visiting during a busy season, grab a bite on the run around 11–11:30. If you have two days for the Magic Kingdom, consider leaving the park at noon and going to one of the hotels for a leisurely, civilized lunch.

Fantasyland—King Stefan's Banquet Hall. Prime ribs, pot pies, and salads are served in a medieval Denny's-style dining hall upstairs in Cinderella's Castle. If you really want to eat here, make reservations as soon as you arrive at the Kingdom.

Liberty Square—Liberty Tree Tavern. Located in the heart of Liberty Square, this colonial New England–themed restaurant serves chowder, sandwiches, and salads for lunch, and more hearty American fare for dinner.

Main Street—Square Cafe. This restaurant in Town Square near Main Street serves breakfast, lunch, and dinner. The menu is simple—pancakes and eggs for breakfast; salads, sandwiches, and barbecued meats for lunch; steaks, ribs, and seafood for dinner. The food is unmemorable but adequate, and the prices are not prohibitively expensive.

Main Street Plaza Restaurant. A bright, art-nouveau-theme restaurant at the end of Main Street where you can get lunch, dinner, or just a treat from the soda fountain.

Aunt Polly's. A nice, peaceful spot on Tom Sawyer Island, where kids can run wild while grownups watch the water and the mainland crowds.

Tomorrowland Terrace. This one-time burgers-only fast-food spot now also has healthy soups and salads.

Epcot Center

The attractions at Epcot are designed more for thoughtful a-dults and curious children than for the fantasy- or thrill-seeking crowd.

The word Epcot stands for Experimental Prototype Communi-ty of Tomorrow—a misleadingly formal title for a park filled with many enjoyable and accessible rides and displays that do more to explain our past and present than to predict the future.

The idea for Epcot was conceived by Walt Disney himself more than 30 years ago. His thought was to create a place that, as he said, "will take its cue from the new ideas and technologies that are now emerging from the creative centers of American indus-try." Disney wanted to be sure that his center kept pace with corporate research and development. It will be, he said, "a community of tomorrow that will never be completed, but will always be introducing and testing and demonstrating new ma-terials and systems." Disney's vision was noble, but what was meant to be a city of tomorrow became little more than a show-case of technology. Still, Future World has enough awe-inspiring attractions to engage even the most incurious of adults and children.

Getting There

Take I–4 west from Orlando to the sign marked Epcot Center. It's about five miles south of the Magic Kingdom exit. If you're coming from the Contemporary, Grand Floridian, or Polyne-sian Village resorts, hop aboard the monorail to the TTC station and follow signs for Epcot. If you're coming from the Magic Kingdom, take the monorail to the TTC and catch the train to Epcot. The 2.5-mile ride from the TTC is enjoyable be-cause the train loops through Future World, Epcot's northern half, providing a dynamic overview of what you'll soon be see-ing and doing. Everybody ooh's and aah's at his first aerial sight of the spectacular grounds.

By Bus From the Disney Inn take the bus with a green pennant to the TTC, then transfer to the Epcot monorail. From Fort Wilder-ness, hop aboard a Blue bus to the TTC. If you're staying at one of the Resort Villas, take the bus with a green-and-gold pen-nant and the letters EC. If you're coming from the Walt Disney World Village Hotel Plaza, take the bus with a silver-and-red pennant.

Parking facilities are as extensive as they are at the Magic Kingdom, and it's easy to forget where you left your car if you're not careful to write down the exact number of the space and the letter of the lot. Trams circle the parking areas. Unlike the trams in the Magic Kingdom, these bring you directly to the turnstiles so there's no need to wait on line for a monorail or ferry.

Orientation

Numbers in the margin correspond with points of interest on the Epcot Center map.

Epcot Center is divided almost equally into two distinct areas separated by the 40-acre World Showcase Lagoon. The northern half, which is where the admission gates are, is filled with the Future World pavilions, sponsored by major American corporations. The southern half is World Showcase.

If you want to minimize time spent waiting on lines, do the opposite of what most people do. In the morning visitors head for what's closest, which is Future World, so you should make a beeline for World Showcase. In the afternoon, come back and explore Future World while the crowds have shifted over to World Showcase. Evening hours, of course, are the best times for visiting either section of Epcot.

Future World

Future World is made up of two concentric circles of modern buildings. The inner circle consists of two crescent-shaped buildings. As you enter, CommuniCore East will be on your left and CommuniCore West will be on your right. The outer circle has seven separate buildings, each featuring a technological theme sponsored by an American corporation.

Be methodical as you visit the attractions in Future World. If you skip around too much you may become disoriented and miss some of the best attractions.

❶ Earth Station—Epcot Information Center. Here, beneath the silvery geosphere, is a sensible place to begin your visit to Epcot. Lunch and dinner reservations can be secured, and questions answered. You can also get maps and entertainment schedules, and arrange for guided tours. Numerous two-way video TV screens, called Worldkey Information Satellites, allow you to see and ask questions of Epcot hosts and hostesses. Merely touch a computer screen and you can summon all sorts of information in several languages. In the Entrance Plaza, before you get to Earth Station, you will find a Sun Bank office, a camera shop, a stroller and wheelchair rental office, and a lost-and-found. Should anyone in your party get lost or separated, he or she should make his way to the Information Desk at Earth Station.

❷ Spaceship Earth. *Very popular; all ages.* This 17-story silver geosphere—some refer to it as a silver golf ball—is the first thing one sees on approaching Epcot. Visible from upper floors of hotels as far as 15 miles away, it is the very symbol of Future World.

Don't let the names confuse you: Earth Station is the Information Center located at the exit to the ride; Spaceship Earth is the ride inside the geosphere itself.

Sponsored by AT&T, Spaceship Earth traces the history of communication. It is a journey through time, beginning with prehistoric wall paintings and continuing through the space age. The familiar voice that narrates your tour belongs to Walter Cronkite. This is one of the most crowded attractions so try to arrive as soon as Epcot opens or late in the evening.

❸ Universe of Energy. *Very popular; all ages.* Sponsored by Exxon, this attraction educates audiences in the origins and different forms of energy. It is called a Traveling Theater because entire rooms shift about as visitors travel through a

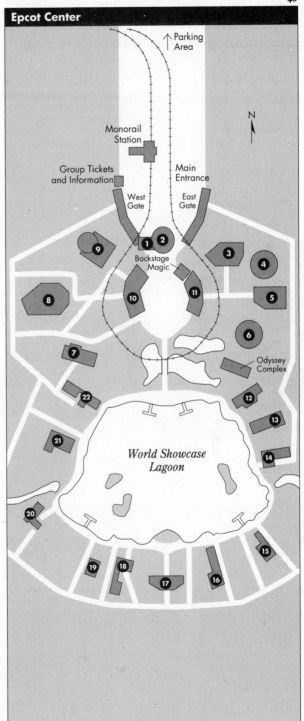

Epcot Center

world of Audio-Animatronics dinosaurs and enter a screening room to learn how energy is created and used.

❹ Wonders of Life. *Popular; all ages.* Housed under a 60-foot gold dome, this newest of Disney's Future World exhibits, sponsored by MetLife, combines a thrill ride, a theater, and hands-on activities. The top attraction is Body Wars, a thrill ride through the immune system of the human body. There is also Cranium Command, a humorous theater show dramatizing the functions of the brain. The Fitness Fairgrounds includes Frontiers of Medicine, exhibits of the latest developments in medicine and health sciences; a Fun House, hands-on learning experiences using the five senses; a Sports Fitness Area, an opportunity to get involved in a variety of electronically enhanced exercise experiences; Goofy about Health, a multiscreen video presentation about good health habits, starring Goofy; Lifestyle Terminals, an opportunity for you to get a computer-generated analysis of your health habits; the Anacomical Players, an improvisational theater troupe that involves guests in humorous skits; and the *Miracle of Life*, a film about human development and birth.

❺ Horizons. *Popular; all ages.* Four-passenger vehicles give visitors a look at the inventions of yesterday, and then convey them into an OmniSphere where on a pair of hemispherical screens they are treated to a look into the world of tomorrow, with scenes of a space shuttle launch, life in a space colony, trains that work by magnetic levitation, and so on. General Electric is the sponsor.

❻ World of Motion. *Moderately popular; all ages.* Sponsored by General Motors, the attraction itself is a rather fanciful, sketchy look at the history of transportation through the ages. The most informative part, Transcenter—you can see it without taking the ride—is a series of displays of vehicles of the future designed by General Motors.

❼ Journey into Imagination. *Popular; for children.* Kids in particular are captivated by the elaborate and colorful trio of attractions that explore the creative process—a ride, a film, and a playground of electric sights and sounds called *Image Works*, where children and adults can exercise their imaginations.

Also in this building is the Captain EO 3-D movie starring pop singer Michael Jackson. There isn't much of a plot to this 17-minute *Star Wars*–type film, but the visual effects are wild. So realistic are the 3-D effects that almost everyone in the audience tries to reach out and touch the images that seem to fly off the screen.

The movie and ride are worth the wait in line, but try to go in the late afternoon when there are less people to contend with. Be sure not to miss the "dancing waters" fountains in front of the entrance to Captain EO. They are especially entertaining after dark.

❽ The Land. Sponsored by Kraft, this building hosts the most educational attractions in Future World for both young and older audiences.

Listen to the Land. Popular; for adults and mature children. The main event in the building is a boat ride through an experimental greenhouse that demonstrates how plants may be grown in the future, not only on Earth but in outer space. This is the most educationally valuable ride in all of Disney World. Some kids may find it dull, but adults are usually impressed. If the experience inspires you to learn more about these processes, you can arrange to join one of the walking tours, guided by professional researchers, that depart a dozen or so times a day. Reservations should be made in the morning on the lower floor, in the corner opposite the boat ride entrance, behind Broccoli and Company (a shop).

Harvest Theatre. Moderately popular; all ages. A beautiful 19-minute nature film called "Symbiosis" shows how people interact with their environment in different ways.

Kitchen Cabaret. Popular; for children. This is a very cute, sunny, Audio-Animatronics show for children about nutrition and the food groups, hosted by Bonnie Appetit and featuring dancing fruits and vegetables, and singing dairy products and meats. Adults with only one day in Epcot may want to skip it. Kids will love it, though.

⑨ The Living Seas. *Popular; all ages.* Venture into the last frontier on Earth as you peer into this massive 5.7-million-gallon aquarium filled with some 8,000 sea creatures, including dolphins and sea lions and the divers who are training them. This serious research facility also features many educational exhibits and interactive displays that inquisitive visitors could spend a good half day exploring.

⑩ ⑪ CommuniCore East and West. These two buildings house exhibits by Epcot's various sponsor companies. There are enough educational computer games to keep an inquisitive mind busy for days, learning how computers work, how energy is generated, how communications systems operate, and much, much more.

Epcot Outreach. This is a resource center in CommuniCore West that provides information and reference material on any subject showcased at Epcot.

World Showcase

World Showcase offers an adventure very different from what you will experience in either the world of the future in Future World or the world of fairytales in the Magic Kingdom. The Showcase presents an ideal image—a Disney version—of life in 11 countries. Native food, entertainment, and wares are on display in each of the pavilions. Most of the nations have done an imaginative and painstaking job of re-creating scale models of their best-known monuments, such as the Eiffel Tower in France, a Mayan temple in Mexico, and a majestic pagoda in Japan. During the day these structures are impressive enough, but at night, when the darkness inhibits one's ability to judge size, one gets the sense that he is seeing the real thing. It's a wonderful illusion, indeed.

Unlike Future World and the Magic Kingdom, the Showcase doesn't offer amusement-park-type rides (except in Mexico and Norway). Instead, it features breathtaking films, ethnic art, cultural entertainment, Audio-Animatronic presentations, and dozens of shops and restaurants featuring national specialities.

You will find that some of the most enjoyable diversions in World Showcase are not inside the national pavilions but in their courtyards and on their streets under the open skies. At varying times of the day, each pavilion offers some sort of live street show, featuring comedy, song, dance, or mime routines, or demonstrations of folk arts and crafts. All performers, craftspeople, and other workers in the pavilions are natives of, or have ancestors from, one of the 11 countries; all are in the U.S. on a cultural exchange program and all speak English and often other languages as well. Don't be shy about exercising or trying to improve your language skills in their native tongues. Teenagers studying French, say, get a charge out of practicing their conversation in France or Morocco.

The only unfortunate note in this cultural smorgasbord is that, with so many shops and restaurants, there seems to be more of an emphasis on commercialism than on education or entertainment. There are many tasteful things to buy, but know in advance that a taste of a nation may mean a bite out of your bank account.

There are three ways of navigating World Showcase: (1) walk from pavilion to pavilion, (2) hop aboard the slow-moving double-decker buses that depart every five to eight minutes and stop in front of every other "nation," or (3) cruise across the lagoon in one of the air-conditioned 65-foot water taxis that depart every 12 minutes. When you first reach the shore of the lagoon closest to Future World, you'll see docks on both your right and your left. The water taxi leaving from the dock on your left travels to the Germany pavilion; the one on the right goes to Morocco. From either stop, you can walk to adjoining pavilions or hop a bus. It's more than a mile around the lagoon, so consider renting strollers for young children, either at the Entrance Plaza to Future World or at the French pavilion (next to Morocco).

The Pavilions The focal point of World Showcase, on the opposite side of the lagoon from the Epcot entrance area, is the host pavilion, the **American Adventure,** sponsored by American Express and Coca-Cola—two symbolic giants of America, both at home and abroad. The pavilions of the other countries fan out from the right and left of American Adventure, encircling the lagoon.

Going clockwise from the left as you enter World Showcase are the pavilions of Mexico, Norway, People's Republic of China, Germany, Italy, American Adventure, Japan, Morocco, France, United Kingdom, and Canada. Apart from the shops and restaurants, here are some of the main attractions at each pavilion.

⑫ **Mexico.** *Not very popular.* The "River of Time" boat ride inside the pavilion may remind some of "It's a Small World" in the Magic Kingdom, with the major tourist attractions of Mexico as its theme. Windows and doorways are filled with colorful video images, rooms are full of dancing, costumed puppets and landscapes that roar, storm, and light up as you journey from the jungles of the Yucatán to the skyline of Mexico City.

The building in which this pavilion is housed is in the form of an ancient Mayan temple similar to those found in the Yucatán. Upon entering the pavilion, visitors pass through a gallery of Spanish colonial art featuring portraits of conquistadores and religious 16th-century artifacts. Inside there is a *mercado* with

colorful textiles, straw items, pottery, other Mexican handi-
crafts, and wandering mariachi bands. In front of the pavilion,
outside, is **Cantina de San Angel**—a fast-food joint and bar
that's good for burritos, margaritas, and—at night—a great
view of the laser show.

⑬ **Norway.** *Popular.* Visitors take a ride in small Viking vessels
through the landscape and history of this Scandinavian country. You can tour a 10th-century Viking Village, sail through a
fjord, and experience a storm and the Midnight Sun.

The main spectacle of this pavilion is a re-creation of a 14th-
century coastal fortress in Oslo called Akershus. Also special is
a film that takes visitors on a tour of the country's architectural
and natural highlights.

⑭ **China.** *Very popular.* The film "Wonders of China" should not
be missed. It is a CircleVision presentation on the landscape of
the country, taking viewers on a fantastic journey from Inner
Mongolia to the Tibetan mountains, along the Great Wall, into
Beijing, and through some of the most glorious landscapes on
Earth.

The Chinese pavilion also features the "House of the Whisper-
ing Willows," an exhibit of ancient Chinese art that is worth
strolling through, and a large shopping gallery, Bountiful Harvest, that is practically a museum in its own right. Browse
among ivory goods, jade jewelry and sculpture, hand-painted
fans, opulent carpets, and inlaid furniture ranging in price
from a few cents to thousands of dollars.

⑮ **Germany.** *Moderately popular.* The main event in this replica
of a small Bavarian village is the oompah band show in the
Biergarten restaurant with singers, dancers, and musicians.
The shops are also worth a quick look. There are four shows daily. You'll also find plenty of German wines, sweets, glassware,
porcelain, and exquisite Christmas-tree ornaments.

⑯ **Italy.** *Moderately popular.* The main event is the archi--
tecture—a reproduction of St. Mark's Square in Venice with
the Campanile (bell tower) di San Marco as its centerpiece and,
behind it, the elegant and elaborately decorated Doges' Palace.
Complementing these buildings are Venetian bridges, gondo-
las, colorful barber poles, and the sculpture of the Lion of St.
Mark atop a column.

In the plaza of this pavilion you can watch and participate in a
comedy show put on by an Italian theater troupe. The broad-
humor farce can be amusing, but only if there is a full, lively audience. At a little shop called Il Bel Cristallo, visitors can watch
artisans at work blowing crystal figurines.

⑰ **American Adventure.** *Popular.* This is a 30-minute Audio-
Animatronics show about the development of the USA. The
huge, Colonial-style theater features the most sophisticated
and realistic Animatronics characters in Disney World. The
show takes visitors from the arrival of the Pilgrims through the
Revolutionary and Civil Wars, the taming of the West, the
World Wars, and so on. The voyage is hosted by Benjamin
Franklin and Mark Twain. Some will find the presentation a bit
long, even though 30 minutes is not much time to cover 200
years of history. Many people find it inspiringly patriotic or
historically skewed, but children may take this opportunity to

catch a few winks—the dramatic music often puts them right to sleep.

Directly opposite the American Adventure pavilion, on the lagoon, is the open-air American Gardens Theater by the Shore, where live, high-energy, all-American shows are performed about four times a day. Show times vary but are posted each day on boards in front of the theater's entrances.

⑱ Japan. *Popular.* Elegant landscaping of rocks, streams, trees, and shrubs combines with traditional architecture to create this peaceful and charming pavilion. Inside the *torii* gates are monumental bronze sculptures of horsemen warriors and a pagoda of five levels, each of which represents one of the five elements of Buddhist belief—earth, water, fire, wind, and sky. Of special interest is the Mitsukoshi Department Store, where lacquered dinnerware, teapots, vases, bonsai trees, and Japanese dolls and toys are for sale; and the Bijutsu-kan Gallery, featuring temporary exhibits of traditional Japanese crafts such as kite-making. The Yakitori House serves inexpensive Japanese fast food in a pleasant garden—a good bet for lunch.

⑲ Morocco. *Popular.* This is one of the more spectacular-looking and exotic of the pavilions. It has a replica of the Koutoubia Minaret from a famous prayer house in Marrakesh; a gallery of Moroccan art, tapestries, and traditional costumes; and a short street with shops selling basketry, leather goods, samovars, exquisite jewelry, and an incredible assortment of metal items. Dancers move to the exotic rhythms of North Africa and get the audience in on the act.

⑳ France. *Popular.* The 18-minute film "Impressions of France" is projected on a five-panel semicircular screen and takes viewers on a romantic tour of France—through the countryside, into the Alps, along the coast, and, of course, into Paris. Viewers will experience the streets of Paris on Bastille Day, the beaches of the Riviera, the gardens of Versailles, and an ascent of the Eiffel Tower. It is a sophisticated adventure with little narration but exquisitely lyrical visuals and classical music.

The pavilion itself resembles a French boulevard lined with shops and cafes. Of special interest are Tout Pour Le Gourmet, and Les Vins de France, two shops featuring French culinary specialties, such as wines, cheeses, mustards, herbs, and pâtés. A little *patisserie/boulangerie* prepares all kinds of baked goods, and two restaurants, Bistro de Paris and Au Petit Cafe, are ideal for lunch. Atop this pavilion is an impressive model of the Eiffel Tower that was constructed using Alexandre Gustave Eiffel's original blueprints.

㉑ United Kingdom. *Moderately popular.* On this street from Old London are a variety of architectural styles from thatched-roof cottages to Tudor and ornate Victorian homes. The city square and rural streets are filled with numerous food, toy, and souvenir shops. The very British Rose and Crown pub serves Stilton cheese, Bass and Guinness ales, and simple English fare. Street actors and a minstrel troupe, the "Pearly Kings and Queens," perform throughout the day, showing the same broad humor as the Italians.

㉒ Canada. *Popular.* A CircleVision film takes its audience into Canada's great outdoors, from the magnificent snow-peaked

Rockies, down sprawling Arctic glaciers, across the plains to Montreal. This thoroughly engaging display makes audiences feel they are experiencing a toboggan run, a dog sled race, and the Calgary Stampede rodeo. Peaceful gardens full of roses, a rocky gorge, emporiums selling everything from sheepskins to lumberjack shirts and maple syrup, and a cafeteria-style restaurant called Le Cellier are other highlights of this quaint pavilion.

Other Attractions in Walt Disney World

Typhoon Lagoon. This 50-acre aquatic entertainment complex features the largest waterslide mountain in the world. The mountain is just under 100 feet high, with nine waterslides shooting down it into white-water rivers and swirling pools. There are huge wave-making lagoons for swimming and surfing.

The water park also includes a Swiss Family Robinson–type tropical island covered with lush greenery, where guests can play at being shipwrecked. A saltwater pool contains a coral reef where snorkelers come mask-to-face with all sorts of Caribbean sea creatures, such as groupers, parrotfish, and even baby sharks.

Disney-MGM Studio Tour. The biggest new addition to Disney World is the Disney-MGM studios, a complete working film production facility that consists of an animation complex, four massive sound stages, a backlot of streets and sets, and numerous film and television post-production facilities, including some of the most technologically advanced special effects studios in the business.

Guests can visit the Animation Building and get a first-hand view of Disney artists at work on the many stages of creating a Disney animated feature. At Video Theater they can participate in the creation of a television show. There are archives full of classic film clips and memorabilia, and a backlot facility filled with costumes in which guests can be photographed.

River Country. In the backwoods setting of the Fort Wilderness Campground Resort, kids can slide, splash, and swim about in an aquatic playground, complete with whitewater inner-tubing channels and corkscrew waterslides that splash down into a 300,000-gallon pond. The pool is heated during the winter so kids can take a dip here all year round. The lake, with its water slides, is too chilly for most swimmers during the winter. In the summer, River Country can get very congested, so it's best to come first thing in the morning. *Fort Wilderness Resort, tel. 407/824–3737. Admission: adults one day $11.75, two days $17.75; children 3–9, one day $9.25, 2 days $13.75. Special tickets are available for admission after 3 PM.*

Discovery Island. Covered with exotic flora, small, furry animals, and colorful birdlife, this little island makes a great escape from the man-made tourist attractions of Disney World. Visitors listen to nature as they stroll along winding pathways, across footbridges, and through one of the biggest aviaries in the United States. Disney did not create these creatures—he just brought them here. Keep an eye out for the Galapagos tortoises, trumpeter swans, scarlet ibis, and bald eagles. It takes less than an hour to walk the trails and see the exhibits, but many visitors stay longer, luxuriating in this respite from the lines and orchestrated activities on the mainland.

Tickets are sold at Fort Wilderness' River Country (just outside the gates of the Magic Kingdom near the turnstiles), at the TTC, at guest service desks in the Disney resorts, and on the island itself. You can get there by watercraft from the Magic

Kingdom, Contemporary Resorts, Polynesian Village, Grand Floridian, and River Country in Fort Wilderness. *Discovery Island: $7.50 adults; $4 children 3–9. River Country/Discovery Island combination ticket: $15 adults; $11 children 3–9.*

4 Exploring Outside Walt Disney World

Numbers in the margin correspond with points of interest on the Exploring Outside Walt Disney World map.

If you feel that you have done all there is to do in Disney World or that you and Mickey need a short vacation from each other, don't despair; there is plenty more to do around Orlando. What you'll discover is that many attractions outside the walls of the Magic Kingdom are equally enjoyable and often less crowded and less expensive.

Each of these other attractions can be seen in one day or less. Just be sure to plan your route with a map. With careful planning, you can group several attractions into one trip and still have time to relax.

General directions are offered here, but it is smart to call in advance for more specific directions tailored to your own itinerary.

❶ Sea World. You may have come to Orlando for Disney World, but it would be goofy not to visit Sea World while you are here. It is the world's largest zoological park, an aquatic wonderland filled with an ocean's worth of sea creatures that perform for you, or that you can pet or simply watch. If you plan your tour of the shows and exhibits when you arrive, you should be able to see the park in about six hours (in time perhaps for some afternoon golf). Of course, you may also want to spend a full day at a more leisurely pace. Organize your visit around the times of the shows, not by the areas they are in. The park is much smaller than it seems on a map and, as you will soon discover, the exhibits are no more than a few minutes' walk from each other. Ask the staff for directions: It can save lots of time. Don't think that, as in Disney World, you will need a week-long pass to see everything here. One day, and an evening if you plan to see the evening shows, is enough. To get a quick overview of the park and the surrounding landscape take a ride up the 400-foot Sky Tower. Cost: $2.50 per person.

A far cry from the little mouse who lives down the road, the mascot of Sea World is a few thousand pounds of affectionate, carnivorous killer whale. Baby Shamu, as she is called, is the most popular feature of the park. The tank that this cute little monster swims in with her parents, aunts, and uncles may seem small but actually is filled with over five million gallons of salt water—give or take a few hundred that have splashed on the onlookers by the end of each show. Shamu impresses her fans with jumps, twists, squirts, and kisses, but be careful not to sit in the first 10 rows of the stadium, especially if you are carrying a camera, unless you enjoy getting drenched.

The two other most entertaining shows are "New Friends," starring whales and dolphins, and "Sea Lions of the Silver Screen," starring a walrus and an otter. These are the funniest, corniest routines in Sea World and are not to be missed.

The newest exhibit in the park is the "Penguin Encounter," featuring more than 200 formally attired aquatic clowns who splash, swim, dive, and gobble fish in a habitat aquarium. The show gets very crowded midday, so try to go in the morning or late afternoon.

Sea World's most elaborate exhibit is the shark tank, where visitors learn about the life cycle and habits of these ravenous

Exploring Outside Walt Disney World

56

Exploring Outside Walt Disney World (detail)

creatures. By the end of your educational, 40-minute underwater tunnel tour, you may even begin to think of these man-eating creatures as friends. "Shark Encounter," a film of a shark's feeding frenzy, is chilling.

If you feel like chumming up to a few sea creatures, buy a few boxes of herring and feed the dolphins, seals, sea lions, and sting rays in their feeding pools. Drop a fish in their mouths as they playfully swim or leap past you. These feeding pools can be the most emotionally rewarding of all the exhibits.

Other presentations include a show demonstrating how animals are trained and a children's show called "Colours in the Dark," performed by Famous People Players, an internationally acclaimed troupe of learning disabled performers. (Adults will enjoy this, too.) Another popular event is the Ski Pirates waterski show, where teams of world-class waterskiers perform acrobatics while skimming the water at high speed.

Every evening Sea World puts on a Polynesian Luau, a dinner show featuring hula dancers, drum music, fire jugglers, and other acts from the islands of the South Pacific. An alternative to the luau is a dinner of alligator meat or some less exotic fare at the Al E. Gator's Restaurant.

7007 Sea World Dr., Orlando 32821, tel. 407/351-3600, in FL 800/432-1178, outside FL 800/327-2424. Open year-round, 9 AM-8 PM with extended hours in the summer. Call for details. Admission: $23.95 adults (weekly pass $26.50); $19.95 children 3-11 (weekly pass $23.50); Polynesian Luau Dinner and Show, 6:45 nightly, $23.27 adults; $16.91 children 8-12; $10.55 children 3-7. Luau reservations tel. in FL 800/227-8048, outside FL 800/ 327-2424. To get there, take I-4 to the Beeline Expressway exit and drive 1 mi to the Sea World/International Dr. Exit. Go to the first traffic light, make a left, and follow signs to one of the parking lots. Parking and dog kennels are free.

❷ Wet 'n Wild. Nothing's better on a hot, sticky, summer day than a cooling dive in the ocean. Unfortunately, the coast is at least a 30-minute drive away, so if you're in a hurry, head to Wet 'n Wild—an aquatic amusement park where you can swim, slide, and play water sports until you shrivel up into a prune. It's conveniently located, just off International Drive. The water slides are better than in River Country, but the environment—a big concrete pool—leaves much to be desired. This of course doesn't bother kids, who are oblivious to the niceties of atmosphere.

The park has over 14 different state-of-the-art water rides, some appealing strictly to children, others to the whole family, and yet others to slide-crazed daredevils. You don't have to know how to swim to enjoy the action because the water depth never exceeds standing height, and there are plenty of brawny, certified lifeguards on duty.

The park has its fair share of snack stands, but visitors are allowed to bring their own food and picnic around the pool or on the lakeside beach. *6200 International Dr. (at Republic Dr.), Orlando, tel. 407/351-3200. Admission: $14.95 adults; $12.95 children 3-12. Open 10-5 PM (sometimes longer). MC, V. Closed Jan.-mid-Feb.*

❸ Universal Studios Florida. Projected to open in the spring of 1990 is the Universal Studios Tour. Brought to you by the makers of *Jaws, King Kong,* and *Conan the Barbarian,* it will feature numerous live-action stunt shows, theatrical and special effects demonstrations, and an adventure tour through mock studios. It will be similar to the Universal Studios Tour in Burbank, CA, where the company is based. *Universal Studios Florida, 1000 Universal Studios Florida, Orlando 32819, tel. 407/363–8000. Admission: about $20 per person.*

Orlando has many smaller attractions that may be of interest to those who want to escape the amusement park world.

(4) In Orlando's Loch Haven Park there is a complex of buildings that feature historical, artistic, and scientific exhibits. The **Orlando Science Center** has science exhibits, the John Young Planetarium's weekend cosmic concerts, a Foucault pendulum, and hands-on displays. *Corner of 17–92 and Princeton, tel. 407/896–7151. Admission: $4 adults, $3 children 4–17, $10 family.*

(5) Next door is the **Orange County Historical Museum** (tel. 407/898–8320), which features exhibits on Orlando's early years and the growth of the orange industry. Admission is free. Behind the museum is a lovingly restored 1926 fire house.

Also in the same complex is the **Orlando Museum of Art** (tel. 407/896–4231), featuring a collection of pre-Columbian art and 19th- and 20th-century paintings. Admission is free for the permanent collection. *Open Tues.–Fri. 10–5, weekends 12–5.*

(6) **Winter Park,** just north of Orlando, is a quaint, fashionable neighborhood with a shopping district full of fancy restaurants, boutiques, and well-known national clothing stores, such as Laura Ashley, Banana Republic, and Ralph Lauren, most of them along Park Avenue.

(7) Just off Park Avenue is the **Charles Hosmer Morse Museum of American Art,** featuring an outstanding collection of stained-glass windows and other decorative arts by Louis Tiffany (son of Charles Tiffany of New York jewelry fame). *133 E. Welbourne Ave., tel. 407/645–5311. Admission: $2.50 adults, $1 children and students. Open Tues.–Sat. 9:30–4, Sun. 1–4.*

(8) Also in this neighborhood is **Rollins College,** an attractive lakeside campus with Spanish-style architecture. On campus is the **Cornell Fine Arts Center** (tel. 407/646–2526), exhibiting 19th-century American paintings from the West as well as a few older European works. *Admission free. Open Tues.–Fri. 9:30–4, Sun. 1–4.*

(9) Each Friday morning you are welcome to attend graduation exercises at the **U.S. Naval Training Center**—one of the nation's largest military training facilities. At 0945 hours sharp, some 600 enlisted men and women pass in review. The Navy Band Orlando plays, the Blue Jacket Chorus sings, and members of the 50-state Flag Team whirl their colorful flags in celebration of the completion of basic training. The exercises take place at Recruit Training Command (General Rees Rd., Orlando, tel. 407/646–4474). There is no admission charge.

(10) Orlando even has its own **Elvis Presley Museum** (tel. 407/345–9427), located in Dowdy Plaza at the intersection of International and Carrier drives. For about $4 (children $3) you can see more than 250 items, including one of Elvis's motorcycles, photographs, jewelry, and other memorabilia from the King.

It's an attractive little shrine that serious fans will not want to miss. *Open daily 9–8.*

⑪ **Boardwalk and Baseball.** This modernized boardwalk-style amusement park was formerly one of Orlando's oldest attractions, Circus World. (Keep in mind that "old" for Orlando means it was built in the 1970s.) Under new ownership, the park was expanded and reopened in 1986 to combine two great American traditions—amusement parks and baseball.

In the tradition of Coney Island and Atlantic City, "B and B" has dozens of dizzying rides that will put you in just about any gravity-defying state you seek—upside down, downside up, you name it. The biggest ride is The Hurricane, one of the South's largest wooden roller coasters, taking riders to speeds up to 60 miles per hour. There are also a dozen or so children's rides, including a traditional merry-go-round, flying space-ships, bumper cars, and so on.

Devotees of America's national sport can exercise their lungs virtually every day of the year. On six playing fields, two of them in small stadiums, there are high school, college, minor league, and major league games. From February to April, the Kansas City Royals hold their spring training here before turning the stadium over to their Class A Florida State League team.

If you feel like testing your own hardball or softball skills, there are numerous professional batting and fielding cages where you can put on a helmet or mitt and check out whether you're major league material. There is also a baseball museum and a film about the sport's greatest players.

Other attractions at the park include a dazzling show featuring Royal Lipizzan stallions. Visitors to the park should not miss the IMAX movie *The Grand Canyon: Hidden Secrets*, which is a mind-boggling film on a six-story-high screen about the history and splendor of one of the world's scenic wonders. The film is almost as exciting as the real thing. *30 minutes from Disney World, at the intersection of I–4 and U.S. 27 in Baseball City, Box 800, Orlando 32802, tel. in Orlando 407/648–5151, in FL 800/367–2249, outside FL 800/826–1939. Admission: $17.95 a-dults, $13.95 children under 4 ft tall and senior citizens over 55. Open summers and major vacation periods, daily 9–9, Sat. 9 AM–11 PM. Off-season times vary; phone for information.*

⑫ **Cypress Gardens.** A visitor can only imagine how glorious and dignified Cypress Gardens must have looked before it was converted into the glitzy amusement playground that it is today. Commercial or not, however, it is still an exceptionally beautiful place. Cypress Gardens is Central Florida's oldest continuously running attraction (yes, even older than Disney World). It was founded as a public botanical garden during the Depression by Dick and Julie Pope. In World War II, when her husband was off serving his country and visitors were few, Julie attracted patrons by dressing the women on her staff in antebellum-style wide hoop skirts and placing them in strategic locations around the gardens. Visitors were so enchanted that these "Flowers of the South" became a tradition as important to the gardens as the tropical blooms themselves.

The gardens are filled with some 8,000 varieties of plants and flowers which bloom year round, tended by a staff of more than 50 horticulturists. While relaxing under the shade of a massive banyan tree you can gaze into a world of tropical and subtropical flora. On the opposite side of the gardens are birds, mammals, and reptiles from all over the globe. There are live alligator shows, a parrot show, and such exotic animals as lemurs, emus, and dromedaries. Children can touch white-tail deer, tortoises, and other tame creatures.

In addition to the flora and fauna are several other attractions including an Ice Palace skating show that children tend to enjoy more than adults. At the Aquacade pool, high divers and synchronized swimmers demonstrate their skills. The biggest event at the gardens is the water-skiing show, a 30-minute revue of high-speed stunts along the shores of Lake Eloise. Don't forget to bring your camera: Cypress Gardens is really a strikingly beautiful place. And don't miss the fireworks and laser light show during extended hours at certain times of the year. *Box 1, Cypress Gardens 33884, tel. 813/324-2111, in FL 800/282-2123, outside FL 800/237-4826. Admission: $16.95 adults, $11.50 children 3-11. Open daily 9-6. To get there, take I-4 west to the U.S. 27 south exit. Follow signs to Winter Haven. When you reach Waverly, turn right (west) on Rte. 540 and drive about 5 mi to the Gardens entrance. It is about a 45-minute drive from Disney World.*

⑬ Bok Tower Gardens. If Cypress Gardens whets your appetite for natural beauty, drive some 20 minutes farther south and enjoy a forest full of plants, flowers, trees, and wildlife native to subtropical Florida.

Bok Tower Gardens is a sanctuary that was designed in 1928 by Frederick Law Olmsted, Jr., son of the famous planner of New York's Central Park. The park was dedicated by President Calvin Coolidge in 1929 to the American people on behalf of Edward Bok, an immigrant from the Netherlands who became a successful New York writer and editor. Shady paths meander through pine forests on a hillside that rises 324 feet above sea level, Florida's highest measured point of land. At the crest of this hill is the 200-foot Bok Singing Tower, made of pink and gray marble covered with intricate latticework. Bronze doors are covered with reliefs of Biblical scenes, and pink and turquoise mosaics depict Florida's exotic wildlife. The tower is a carillon with 53 bronze bells that ring every half-hour. Each day at 3 PM there is a 45-minute recital; depending on when you are there, you may hear Early American folk songs, Appalachian tunes, Irish ballads, Latin hymns, and so on. There are also moonlight recitals and special programs with visiting artists. This world of silvery moats, mockingbirds and swans, blooming thickets, and hidden sundials will be a welcome retreat from the land of highways, malls, and amusement parks. *Box 3810, Lake Wales, 33853, tel. 813/676-1408. Admission: $2 Adults, children under 12 free. Open daily 8-5. To get there, continue past the Cypress Gardens turnoff on U.S. 27 for about 5 mi, turn off on Rte. 17A to Alt. U.S. 27. Follow signs past the orange groves, through the town of Lake Wales, to the park.*

⑭ Gatorland Zoo. This is an unusual attraction that features over 400 alligators and 40 crocodiles swimming and basking in the sun in a swampy lake. There's also a nursery with thousands of alligators crawling all over each other and a zoo that houses many other reptiles, in addition to monkeys, farm animals, and even a tapir.

The main event at the zoo takes place four times a day. It's called the Gator Jumparoo. A zoo keeper dangles a whole chicken four feet over the water, and on command a gator or two will leap—yes, actually leap—out of the water and swallow the chicken whole. It is not exactly a circus of performing alligators, but it is fun to watch. The best jumparoo of the day is the first one in the morning, when the beasts are hungriest. *14501 S. Orange Blossom Trail, Orlando 32821, tel. 407/855-5496. Open daily 8 AM-6 PM. Admission: $5.40 adults, $3.95 children 3-11. To get there from I-4 in Orlando, take the Kissimmee Exit and drive south on Orange Blossom Trail (U.S. 441, 17-92) for about 10 miles. From the Disney-Kissimmee area, exit I-4 at Irlo Bronson Memorial Hwy. (U.S. 192), and take the Orange Blossom Trail north.*

15 Tupperware World Headquarters. Less than a mile from Gatorland is the home of the world's biggest Tupperware party. Here at Tupperware's corporate headquarters, visitors are given a free 25-minute tour of a display kitchen, living room, playroom, and trailer home demonstrating the boundless versatility of those famous plastic products that "aren't just for cooking anymore." *U.S. 441, Box 2353, Orlando 32802, tel. 407/847-3111. Open Mon.-Fri., 9-4. Tours every 30 minutes.*

16 Florida Citrus Tower. Advertised extensively around Orlando, this is said to be the highest observation point in the state, where you can gaze over thousands of acres of orange trees. If you go to the upper, outside observation deck and put a quarter in a telescope, you will see even more acres of orange trees. If the view inspires you to learn about the citrus industry and about different varieties of oranges, you can sign up for tours of the grove. There are also citrus candy and marmalade factories, and a glassblower's workshop. *On U.S. 27 in Clermont, 1 mi north of Rte. 50, about 45 minutes west of Orlando. Tel. 904/394-8585. Open 7 AM-6 PM. Admission: $2.50 adults, $1.75 children 10-15.*

17 Busch Gardens. If you have seen all of Orlando's amusement parks and are still looking for more action, Busch Gardens, only a 75-minute drive from Disney World, is a "must see." It is the second most popular tourist attraction in the entire state and for good reason. It is an imaginatively and convincingly designed turn-of-the-century African theme park for more than 3,000 animals, with an emphasis on breeding endangered species and creating natural habitats.

The Moroccan-style architecture alone is worth a visit. Huts, tents, and bazaars filled with imported goods make visitors feel they have stumbled onto an African stage set. The stadium where the Sea World–type "Dolphins of the Deep" show is presented is inspired by the traditional architecture of Timbuktu.

Although there are many things to see and do, the park's real draw is its animals. There is an extensive children's petting zoo and habitat displays for all sorts of animals. Tigers pace a tropical island, crocodiles bask in swamps, elephants spray themselves in a rocky cave, and antelopes, zebras, camels, and countless other quadrupeds graze on 60 acres of savannah.

One of the most fascinating attractions is the World of Birds. This is the most impressive bird show in Florida and should not be missed. Birds you can see up close include a bald eagle and a golden eagle—two of the most noble creatures on earth; countless owls, vultures, and parrots; and a condor so big that it is kept on a leash.

After you've seen the animals, take a tour through the Budweiser brewery (an Anheuser-Busch brewery). Or take a few spins on the two teeth-clenching, corkscrew roller coasters. Busch Gardens may be a significant drive from Orlando, but few visitors regret the trip. *300 E. Busch Blvd. at 40th St., Tampa, tel. 813/971–8282. Admission for adults and children, $19.95. Parking $2. Open daily 9:30–6. Extended hours during the summer and selected holidays; phone for details. To get there, take I–4 west to Tampa and exit at I–75. Take Exit 54 and follow signs to the park.*

⑱ Spaceport USA. The Kennedy Space Center is free, making it perhaps the best entertainment bargain in Florida. You can stroll through an outdoor rocket garden with authentic rockets and tour a museum filled with spacecraft that have explored the last frontier. There are also two bus tours: One takes visitors to see some of NASA's current launch facilities, including the Space Shuttle launch. Another bus goes to Cape Canaveral Air Force Station, where you can trace the history of the early space program. Understandably, some visitors are less than thrilled about viewing the space program framed through a bus window. There is both live and recorded narration, but most sights are experienced from afar, except for historical exhibits at camera stops.

The one event that should make your entire trip to Spaceport worthwhile (if you have not already experienced it at the Air and Space Museum in Washington, DC) is the IMAX film *The Dream Is Alive.* Projected onto a five-and-a-half-story screen, this 40-minute film takes you from astronaut training through a thundering shuttle launch, into the cabins and life on board the shuttle during flight, and back to Earth for touchdown. The footage shot by the astronauts themselves will leave you breathless. It is a completely overwhelming experience, costing only a few dollars for the whole family. *Kennedy Space Center, FL 32899, tel. 407/452–2121. Bus tours: $4 adults, $1.75 children 3–12. IMAX film: $2.75 adults, $1.75 children. No credit cards. Open daily 9 AM–dark. Last tour 2 hours before dark. Closed Christmas Day and certain launch dates. Kennedy Space Center is about a 90-minute drive from Disney World and a 60-minute drive from Orlando. To get there, take the Beeline Expressway (off I–4) east for about 25 min. to Rte. 407. Go east to Rte. 405, then east again, following signs to Spaceport. Parking and kennel facilities are free.*

⑲ Spirit Country. For a totally different sort of experience, head north of Orlando to the town of Cassadaga, which possesses one of the nation's largest communities of psychic mediums. Leave behind your notions of gypsies huddled over crystal balls; most members of the Cassadaga Spiritualist Camp are reclusive and formally certified by one of various national spiritualist associations. Many are ordained ministers of the Spiritualist Church. These mediums communicate with your spirits and the spirits of others primarily for purposes of "healing"—not as in mending broken bones but as in healing a sickness of the soul. They believe in communication with the dead and assert that supernatural experiences such as clairvoyance, levitation, and materialization are functions of everlasting spirits. And when you listen to them talk, it all sounds believable.

The camp welcomes visitors who wish either to sit in on one of the unusual Sunday church services (usually held from 10:30 to 11:30 AM) or to get a "reading" from one of the camp members. You are expected to find a medium who is right for you by walking or driving through this rustic, five-by-five-block neighborhood and stopping at the house that seems to be giving off the right sort of energy. You're expected to take the experience seriously. "Don't move the spirit," as one medium said, "unless the spirit needs moving." It sounds like good advice.

Whether you take the advice or not, it is worth a trip here just to walk around the serene, wooded camp, attend a church service, and learn more about spiritualism from the materials in the book-shop located on Stevens Street (Open Mon.–Sat. 9–5, Sun. noon–4), or from talking to some of the mediums. The people here are friendly and wholesome; all they ask of visitors is that they dress appropriately and treat the site with respect (in other words, don't litter). *Box 319, Cassadaga 32706, tel. 904/228–2880. The Cassadaga Spiritualist Camp is about 35 mi north-east of Orlando. To get there, take I–4 to Exit 54 for Lake Helen and Cassadaga.*

5 Shopping

Shopping is part of the entertainment in both the Magic Kingdom and Epcot Center. There's something in every price range
in virtually every store, so even kids on allowances can get in on
the act. Shops of special interest within Walt Disney World are
discussed in the Exploring section. What follows is a look at the
shopping opportunities in the greater Orlando area.

Orlando is packed with malls. They are everywhere. It is virtually impossible to step outside your hotel room without seeing a
mall or a sign advertising one. You'll find everything from shopping complexes to flea markets, factory outlets, specialty
stores, department stores, and gift shops. The area provides a
great opportunity to do a lifetime of shopping in a few days.

Almost all malls and outlets are open Monday to Saturday from
9 to 7 and on Sunday from 11 to 7. Most stores accept traveler's
checks and major credit cards.

Factory Outlet Malls

The International Drive area is lined with factory outlet stores,
most of them on the northeast end. These outlets are clumped
together in expansive malls or scattered along the Drive. Much
of the merchandise is discounted from 20% to 75%. You can find
just about anything, some of it top quality. But be advised,
these are not charming places to shop. Most of you will want to
make your purchases and continue on your way.

Belz Factory Outlet Mall and Annexes. This is the largest collection of outlet stores—nearly 100—located in a mall and in two
nearby annexes. The atmosphere is "bargain basement," but
it's possible to come away with some good buys. Outlets include
Danskin, London Fog, Bally Shoes, Bass Shoes, Anne Klein,
Carol Hochman (featuring Christian Dior), Van Heusen, Big R
(featuring Rawlings sporting goods), Fieldcrest, Cannon, and
Calvin Klein. *5401 W. Oakridge Rd., Orlando (at the northern
tip of International Dr.), tel. 407/352–9611.*

Quality Outlet Center and Quality Center East. These are two
interconnected malls with 21 brand-name factory outlet stores
including American Tourister, Great Western Boots, Corning/
Revereware, Royal Doulton, Jonathan Logan, and Mikasa (dinnerware). *5409 and 5529 International Dr. (1 block north of
Kirkman Rd.), tel. 407/423–5885.*

Denim World. A great place for Levi's, Lee, Activewear, and so
on, always on sale. Often two-for-one deals, as well. You may
have a hard time finding your size, but there are free altera-
tions while you wait. Bring a book and you may just finish it.
7623 International Dr., tel. 407/351–5704.

Edwin Watts Golf Shop. A no-handicap shop for golfing equipment. *7220 International Dr., tel. 407/345–8451.*

Dansk Factory Outlet. All the dinnerware, flatware, glassware, cookware you can imagine—and all at discount prices.
7000 International Dr., tel. 407/351–2425.

China Arts and Crafts. The People's Republic of China's largest
outlet in the United States. Full of arts and crafts, vases,
bowls, and so on. Hardly museum pieces, but much cheaper
than the china at Epcot. *8445 International Dr., tel. 407/351–
2626.*

Flea Markets

When you see signs for flea markets, remember that most are nothing but collections of shops run by small-time retailers. Bargains are possible on all sorts of bric-a-brac.

Flea World. It claims to be America's largest flea market under one roof. It just might be! There are 1,200 booths, and two new structures and another row in the original building have recently been added. There is plenty here that you may want, but only after wading through piles of junk. You can find everything from rabbits to samurai swords and costume jewelry. *30 minutes north of Orlando (I–4 to Exit 50, east to Hwy. 17-92, then right 1 mi), tel. 407/645–1792. Open Fri.–Sun., rain or shine, 8–5.*

Malls/Department Stores

National department stores are scattered throughout the city, but two large malls in particular are likely to carry whatever you are looking for.

The Florida Mall. This shopping complex includes Sears, J.C. Penney's, Belk Lindsey, Maison Blanche, and 167 specialty shops. *8001 S. Orange Blossom Trail, Orlando (4½ miles east of I–4 and International Dr.), tel. 407/851–6255.*

Altamonte Mall. Another massive mall with more than 150 stores, including Sears, Maison Blanche, Jordan Marsh, and Burdine's department stores, as well as 165 specialty shops. *451 Altamonte Ave., Altamonte Springs (½ mi east of I–4 on Rte. 436), tel. 407/830–4400.*

Shopping Villages

These are quaint, themed shopping centers filled with gift shops, clothing stores, and restaurants. They are primarily for tourists, with tourist prices, but they are much more pleasant and relaxed than the malls.

Walt Disney World Shopping Village. This is the site of WDW's largest character merchandise shops and source for everything from Christmas tree ornaments to toys, china, and state-of-the-art coffee grinders. The prices are no better or worse than they are anywhere in the country. Disney clothing, stuffed animals, and souvenirs abound in more than 20 shops. It is relatively quiet during the early part of the day, but can get busy in the afternoons and evenings. While parents shop, kids can rent boats at the marina, which is right there. *Lake Buena Vista, tel. 407/828–3058. Open daily 10 AM–10 PM.*

Church Street Exchange. This is a decorative, brassy, Victorian-themed "festival marketplace" filled with more than 60 specialty shops. Lots of old-fashioned shopping for old-fashioned tastes. *Church St. Station, 129 W. Church St., tel. 407/422–2434. Open 11 AM–2 AM.*

Mercado Mediterranean Shopping Village. Spanish-style architecture houses over 60 specialty shops featuring all sorts of gifts from Chinese pottery to broadswords from Toledo (Spain, that is). The courtyards are filled with fine restaurants such as

Altamonte Mall, **9**
Belz Factory Outlet, **1**
China Arts, **6**
Church Street, **11**
Dansk, **5**
Denim World, **3**
Edwin Watts Golf, **4**
Eli's Orange World, **16**
Flea World, **7**
Florida Mall, **8**
Mercado, **12**
Marketplace, **13**
Old Town, **14**
Park Ave., **15**
Quality Outlet, **2**
WDW Shopping
Village, **10**

Shopping

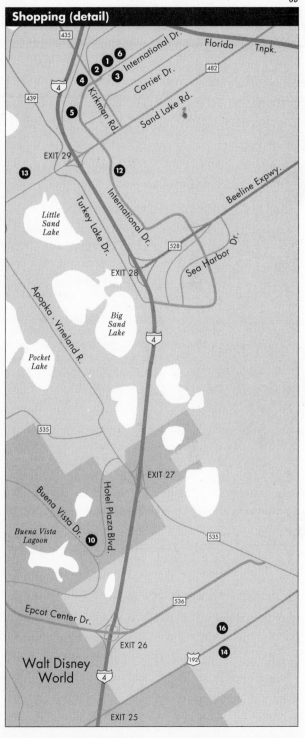

Shopping (detail)

435

International Dr.

Florida Tnpk.

6
1
2
3
Carrier Dr.
4
482

4

Sand Lake Rd.

439

Kirkman Rd.

5

EXIT 29

13

12

Turkey Lake Dr.

International Dr.

Beeline Expwy.

Little Sand Lake

528

Sea Harbor Dr.

EXIT 28

Apopka - Vineland R.

Big Sand Lake

4

Pocket Lake

535

EXIT 27

Buena Vista Dr.

Hotel Plaza Blvd.

535

Buena Vista Lagoon

10

536

Epcot Center Dr.

16

EXIT 26

14

192

Walt Disney World

4

EXIT 25

Royal Orleans, Mardi Gras, and **Paulo's** for lunch. *8445 International Dr., tel. 407/345-9337. Open daily 10 AM-10 PM.*

The Marketplace. This outdoor shopping center is super convenient for taking care of all your basic necessities in one spot. Stores include a pharmacy, post office, one-hour film processor, stationery and card store, bakery, and 24-hour supermarket. Also in the Marketplace are two good restaurants: **Christini's** (tel. 407/345-8770) and **Darbas** (tel. 407/345-8128). *7600 Dr. Phillips Blvd., Orlando, tel. 407/351-7000. Take I-4 or International Dr. to Sand Lake Rd. It is two stoplights west of the I-4 Sand Lake exit.*

Old Town. A well-designed, turn-of-the-century, old-Florida-theme complex with brick streets and historical architecture—a good bet for visitors to the Kissimmee area. Shops feature all sorts of crafted items such as quilts, ceramic tiles, and religious wood carvings. There is an ice cream parlor, coffee shop, candy store, and a 1950s nostalgia nightclub, **Little Darlin's.** *5770 Irlo Bronson Memorial Hwy., Kissimmee (east of I-4), tel. 407/396-4888. Open daily 10 AM-10 PM.*

Park Avenue. This posh shopping district in historic Winter Park is lined with many famous stores. The smells of roasted coffee beans, French perfumes, and fresh-baked chocolate chip cookies assault you as you walk down Park Avenue, past galleries, antiques shops, and stores such as Banana Republic, Benetton, The Gap, Orvis, Laura Ashley, and Ralph Lauren. Since local residents are the prime clientele, there's a real-world aura here that's refreshing.

Eli's Orange World. Ship home oranges from this 10,000-acre grove. *4 mi east of Disney World on Rte. 192, tel. 407/396-1306.*

6 Sports and Fitness

Participant Sports

Golf and Tennis Many resort hotels let nonguests use their golf and tennis facilities. Some hotels are affiliated with a particular country club, offering preferred rates. If you are staying near a resort with facilities you want to use, call and inquire about their policies. Be sure always to call in advance to reserve courts and tee times. What follows is a list of the best places open to the public.

Golf **Golfpac** (Box 484, Maitland 32751, tel. 407/660–8559) packages golf vacations and prearranges tee-times at over 25 courses around Orlando.

Walt Disney World's three championship courses—all on the PGA Tour route—are among the busiest and most expensive in the region. Greens fees are $45 for guests staying in Disney World properties, $55 for nonguests, and $25 after 3 PM.

Golf lessons are given in small groups at the two Disney Inn courses, the Magnolia and the Palm. Private lessons are available both at these courses and at the Lake Buena Vista Club. There is also a nine-hole, 1,115-yard course on artificial turf with natural turf greens for children ($7) and adults ($9). For private lessons at the Lake Buena Vista Club, phone 407/828–3741. For all other information, phone 407/824–2270.

Poinciana Golf & Racquet Resort (500 Cypress Pkwy., tel. 407/933–5300) has a par-72 course about 18 miles southeast of Disney World.

Tennis **Disney Inn** has two courts, **Lake Buena Vista Club** has three, **Fort Wilderness Campground** has two, and the **Contemporary Resort Hotel** has six. Private and group lessons are available at the Contemporary (tel. 407/824–3578). Racquets can be rented by the hour.

Orange Lake Country Club (tel. 407/239–1050) offers golf, inexpensive tennis, and a variety of water sports. Greens fees $48, tennis $4 per hour.

Health Clubs **Justus Aquatic Center** (Radisson Inn, 8444 International Dr., Orlando, tel. 407/345–0505) has nautilus, freeweights, racquetball, tennis, tanning, and more. $8 for all facilities; $8 an hour extra for racquetball, $12 after 5 PM.

Water Sports Marinas at **Caribbean Beach Resort, Contemporary Resort, Fort Wilderness, Polynesian Village, Grand Floridian,** and **Walt Disney World Shopping Village** rent sunfish, catamarans, motor-powered pontoon boats, pedal boats, and tiny two-passenger Water Sprites—a hit with kids—for use on Bay Lake, the adjoining Seven Seas Lagoon, Club Lake, Lake Buena Vista, or Buena Vista Lagoon. The Polynesian Village marina rents outrigger canoes. Fort Wilderness rents canoes for paddling along the placid canals in the area. For water-skiing reservations ($65 per hour), phone 407/824–2222, ext. 2757.

Airboat Rentals (4266 Vine St., Kissimmee, tel. 407/847–3672) rents airboats ($15.99 an hour) and canoes for use on the Shingle Creek, with views of giant cypress trees and Spanish moss.

Ski Holidays (tel. 407/239–4444) has water skiing, jet-skiing, and parasailing on a private lake next to Disney World. Boats $50 per hour, $180 for 4 hours. Parasailing $30. To get there, take I–4 to the Lake Buena Vista exit, turn east on Rte. 535 toward Kissimmee, and about 200 yards east you will see a sign to Lake Bryan.

Rent a powerful seven-seater ski boat at **Sanford Boat Rentals** (tel. 407/321–5906, in FL 800/237–5105, outside FL 800/692–3414) and travel up the St. John's River. Bring your own equipment for bass fishing or rent water-ski equipment. Very good rates for whole-day outings. Houseboats and pontoons are available for day, overnight, weekend, or week-long trips. Pontoon and ski boats $60 for 4 hours; 44-foot houseboat $350 per day, $560 for 2 days, $450 weekends, $900 weekly. Rates vary seasonally.

Three Buoys Houseboat Rentals (2280 Hontoon Dr., DeLand, tel. 904/736–9422 or 800/262–3454) rents luxury houseboats on the St. Johns River. Among the packages is a $695 weekend deal and a weekly price of $1,195. Rates vary seasonally.

Fishing **Fort Wilderness Campground** (tel. 407/W–DISNEY) is the starting point for two-hour fishing trips, departing at 8 AM and 3 PM. Boat, equipment, and guide for up to five anglers costs $110.

Central Florida is covered with freshwater lakes and rivers teaming with all kinds of fish, from largemouth black bass to perch, catfish, sunfish, and pike. If you have your own equipment and need only a boat and bait, the place to go is Lake Tohopekaliga. For information, advice, and equipment, call **Hook, Line and Sinker Bait and Tackle Shop** (307A E. Broadway, Kissimmee, tel. 407/847–9310).

Bass Challenger Guide (726 Ashley Ct., Orlando, tel. 407/273–8045) rents Ranger Boats equipped with drinks and tackle. Transportation can be arranged to and from their location. Half-day (one or two persons) from $110, full day from $160.

Bass Bustin' Guide (5935 Swoffield Dr., Orlando, tel. 407/281–0845) provides boat, tackle, transportation, and amenities for bass fishing on local lakes. And they guarantee fish! Half day from $125, full day from $150.

Bicycling The most scenic bike riding in Orlando is on Disney World property, along roads that take you past forests, lakes, golf courses, and Disney's wooded resort villas and campgrounds. Bikes are available for rent at **Caribbean Beach Resort** (tel. 407/934–3400), **Fort Wilderness Bike Barn** (tel. 407/824–2742), and **Walt Disney World Village Villa Center** (tel. 407/824–6947). Bike rental $3 an hour, $7 per day.

Jogging Walt Disney World has several scenic jogging trails. Pick up jogging maps at any Disney resort. **Fort Wilderness** (tel. 407/824–2900) has a 2.3-mile jogging course with plenty of fresh air and woods as well as numerous exercise stations along the way.

Horseback Riding **Grand Cypress Resort Equestrian Center** (tel. 407/239–1234) offers hunter/jumper private lessons, and riding trails for guided outings. Private lesson $35 an hour, trailside $20 an hour.

Fort Wilderness Campground Resort (tel. 407/W–DISNEY) in Disney World offers tame trail rides through backwoods and along lakesides. Open to the general public. Call in advance to arrange an outing. Rides at 9, 10:30, noon, and 2. Cost is $10 per person for 45–60 minutes. Children must be over nine.

Ice Skating **Orlando Ice Skating Palace** (3123 W. Colonial Dr., Parkwood Shopping Plaza, Orlando, tel. 407/299–5440) isn't the most attractive rink, but if you are homesick for a winter chill, this should do the trick. Open Wed.–Sun. 7:30–10:30 PM. Call for daytime hours.

Spectator Sports

Jai Alai **Orlando–Seminole Jai–Alai.** The sport is fun to watch even if you don't bet. *$1 general admission, $2 reserved seating. Open May–mid-Jan. at 7:20 nightly except Sun. with noon matinees Mon., Thurs., and Sat. Fern Park, off I–4 about 20 minutes north of Orlando, tel. 407/331–9191.*

Dog Racing **Sanford Orlando Kennel Club** (301 Dog Track Rd., Longwood, tel. 407/831–1600) has dog racing and betting nightly at 7:45 *PM* except Sunday. *Matinees Mon., Wed., and Sat. at 1 PM. Admission $1. Open Nov.–May.*

Seminole Greyhound Park (2000 Seminola Blvd., Casselberry, tel. 407/699–4510) is a newer track with racing nightly at 7:45 except Sunday. *General admission $1, clubhouse $2, children halfprice. Open May–Oct. Weekday matinees have been changing times each year, most recently they have been 3 PM Tues. and Wed. and 1 PM Sat.*

Basketball **Orlando Magic** (Box 76, Orlando, FL 32802, tel. 407/89–MAGIC) joined the National Basketball Association in the 1989–90 season. The team plays in the new, 16,000-seat Orlando Arena. *Admission $8–$17. Exit I–4 at Amelia, the arena is two blocks west of the interstate.*

Baseball The **Orlando Twins** are Minnesota's Class AA Southern League affiliate. They play baseball at Tinker Field. *Exit I–4 at Colonial Ave. (Hwy. 50), go west to Tampa Ave. and south on Tampa to the stadium. Tel. 407/849–6346.*

The **Osceola Astros** are Houston's Class A team in the Florida State League. They play at Osceola County Stadium in Kissimmee. *Tel. 407/933–5500.*

The **Baseball City Royals** are Kansas City's Class A team in the Florida State League. They play at Boardwalk and Baseball, where you can get combination tickets for the park and game. *Tel. 407/648–5151.*

Soccer **Orlando Lions** play in the American Soccer League. Games are April through Aug. at Orlando Stadium weekends at 7:30 PM. *Admission $6. The stadium is adjacent to Tinker Field (see Orlando Twins, above).*

7 Dining

Many of Orlando's finest restaurants are located in the stylish hotels in the heavily touristed areas. These dining establishments like to flaunt their sophisticated menus and wine lists, and show off their big-city tastes. The thing is, many of them actually are as good as one can expect from the best chain hotel restaurants anywhere in the United States. If you want convenience, decent food, and a cosmopolitan atmosphere, hotel restaurants are a safe bet. If, however, you're watching your pennies or enjoy an atmosphere with a certain regional flavor, try some local spots in Orlando. You may have to drive to find a restaurant with much character, but you'll be rewarded with a taste of Orlando, and considerable savings.

The dress code is indicated after each restaurant's address below. Ties are always optional, though men on the far side of 30 commonly wear them. "Casual," which applies to all but the fanciest place in Orlando, means comfortably presentable—avoiding shorts, sneakers, and T-shirts. "Informal" means wear whatever you please.

It is always a good idea to make reservations, even on a slow night; otherwise a large group may arrive moments before you, and keep you waiting on line. Orlando is not a big town, but getting to places is almost always complicated, so always call for directions. The budget-conscious should consider dining before 6 PM, when many area restaurants offer early-bird specials.

If you want to try some local specialties, consider stone crabs, pompano (a mild white fish), Apalachicola oysters, small tasty Florida lobsters, and conch chowder. Fresh hearts of palm are a treat, too.

The most highly recommended restaurants in each price category are indicated by a star ★.

Category	Cost*
Very Expensive	over $40
Expensive	$30–$40
Moderate	$20–$30
Inexpensive	under $20

*per person without tax, service, or drinks

The Walt Disney World Area

These are restaurants close to Disney World, situated along International Drive or near Kissimmee, Disney Maingate, and Lake Buena Vista.

American **Empress Lilly.** Disney's 220-foot, 19th-century Mississippi-style riverboat is a popular tourist dining spot permanently moored at the far end of Walt Disney World Shopping Village, right on Buena Vista Lagoon. Though its bright red paddle wheel has never moved the boat an inch, much attention was paid to make it look like an elegant, old-fashioned Victorian showboat, complete with brass lamps, burgundy velvet loveseats, and mahogany wood. The boat has several restaurants and lounges. Beef is served in Steerman's Quarters, and seafood in Fisherman's Deck. Only 5% of the tables are open for reservations, two days in advance. Visitors without reservations should arrive early, add their names to the list, and go and listen to banjo music in Baton Rouge Lounge. The food is as predictable as it is expensive, but dining here can be a fun, enjoyable experience for large families or groups that want a decent meal but do not want to feel inhibited by a stuffy atmosphere. The third restaurant on the showboat is the Empress Room, a plush, Louis XV-style dining room filled with gilded reminders of another age. It is a small, luxurious (if gaudy) setting that might bring out the Rhett Butler or Scarlett O'Hara in you, but you will wish that the food measured up to the prices. The menu reads elegantly, featuring such specialties as duck, pheasant, venison, and various seafood dishes—but the food is unlikely to live up to expectations suggested by the elegance of the setting. *Steerman's Quarters and Fisherman's Deck: Walt Disney World Shopping Village, tel. 407/828-3900. Dress: casual. Only a few reservations accepted. AE, MC, V. Moderate. Empress Room: Jacket required. Reservations required, up to a month in advance. AE, DC, MC, V. Expensive.*

Australian **The Outback.** A glass elevator descends into this huge restaurant beside a waterfall and pool, located behind the Buena Vista Palace Hotel. In the middle of the room are the grills and barbecue pits where the chefs cook up "surf and turf" Aussie specialties such as rack of lamb and lobster tail. Ninety-nine brands of beer are served in this fun, relaxed family restaurant, where waiters serve you in Outback safari outfits and the kids don't have to sit on their hands. *Buena Vista Palace, Walt Disney World Village, Lake Buena Vista, tel. 407/827-3430. Dress: casual. Reservations accepted. AE, MC, V. Moderate.*

Cajun/Creole **Royal Orleans.** This is some of the most authentic Louisiana cooking you will find outside of New Orleans, prepared under the direction of an award-winning Cajun chef, "Beany" MacGregor. When the British owner decided to open a New Orleans–theme restaurant and dinner theater named Mardi Gras, he went to Louisiana to get the best Cajun chef he could find. Beany MacGregor consented to return with him to Orlando, but only on the condition that he could open a restaurant of his own. Royal Orleans is that restaurant. You can find some of Beany's award-winning Cajun recipes on the menu, such as sherried turtle soup and *truite roulée* (small slivers of trout filet, shrimp, Louisiana blue crab, and fresh artichoke hearts wrapped in spinach leaves and topped with Béarnaise sauce). Much of the fresh seafood and crawfish are flown in daily from Louisiana. Reading the menu is the next best thing to a class in Louisiana's culture and cuisine. Royal Orleans is located in the back left corner as you drive into the Mercado Shopping Village on International Drive. *8445 International Dr., Orlando, tel. 407/352-8200. Jackets required. Reservations advised. AE, DC, MC, V. Moderate.*

Chinese **Haifeng.** This is not your typical Chinese dinner, but outstand-
★ ing, traditional Hunan fare. The ingredients are so fresh and the preparation so attentive that even a simple spring roll becomes a new taste treat. Both the service and the decor are elegant. The specialties are seafood delight soup, Szechuan snapper, and an Imperial Duck that looks too good to be eaten. Dinner at Haifeng is a quiet and civilized affair that should be enjoyed at a leisurely pace. *Stouffer Resort, 6677 Sea Harbor Dr., Orlando, tel. 407/351-5555. Jackets requested. Reser-*

Dining *

Arthur's 27, **6**
Atlantis, **7**
Bee Line Diner, **16**
Bubble Room, **17**
Capriccio, **11**
Cattle Ranch, **24**
Chalet Suzanne, **18**
Christini's, **12**
Coq au Vin, **20**
Darbar, **10**
Dux, **8**
Empress Lilly, **2**
Haifeng, **5**
Hemingway's, **15**
La Coquina, **9**
Outback, **3**
Palm Terrace, **14**
Park Plaza Gardens, **19**
Ran-Getsu, **13**
Rossi's, **22**
Royal Orleans, **4**
Skeeter's, **25**
South Seas, **23**
Victoria and Albert's, **1**
Villa Las Palomas, **21**

* All restaurants
except those in
Epcot Center

0   1 mile

0   1 km

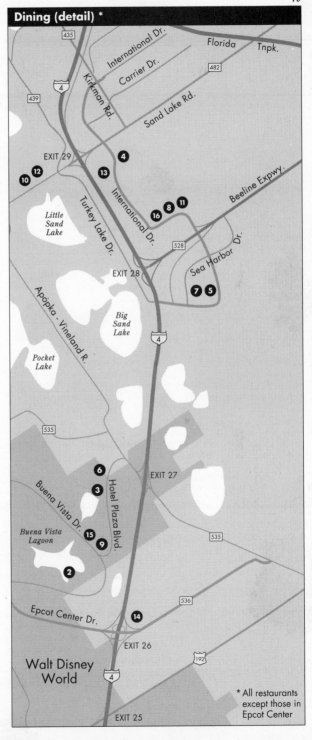

vations recommended. *AE, CB, DC, MC, V. Moderate–Expensive.*

Continental   **Arthur's 27.** Situated on the top floor of the Buena Vista Palace Hotel, visitors to Arthur's 27 get not only an elegant meal but also one of the best views of the Magic Kingdom and Epcot. The fixed-price, seven-course Continental dinner will set you back $55 per person, *without* drinks; if you order à la carte, expect to pay more. Service and quality are first class, though bordering on the pretentious. The wine list is formidable, featuring everything from reasonable California wines to some vintage Bordeaux that could be sold at auction. Specialties include venison and sautéed breast of duck with honey ginger sauce. Arthur's is very popular on weekends, so reservations are strongly suggested. There is only one seating per night, so reservations are at a premium and should be made at the same time that you reserve your room. Dinners last several hours, so make sure you're with someone you like. *Buena Vista Palace Hotel, Walt Disney World Village, tel. 407/827–3450. Jackets required. Reservations strongly recommended. AE, CB, DC, MC, V. Very Expensive.*

Victoria and Albert's. A small but very elegant gourmet restaurant, located at Disney's Grand Floridian Beach Resort, where guests dine on Royal Doulton china with Sambonet silver from Italy and Schott-Zweisel crystal from Germany. There is no menu but you can expect to pay about $65 for a prix-fixe fare chosen from fish, fowl, red meat, veal, and lamb. What you get is appetizer, soup, entree, salad, a plate of fruit and cheese accompanied by a glass of port, and dessert. Guests are served by "maids" and "butlers" named Victoria and Albert, and after dinner women receive a long-stemmed American Beauty rose. There are only 53 seats, and smoking is not allowed. *Grand Floridian, Walt Disney World, tel. 407/824–2383. Jackets required. Reservations required. AE, MC, V. Very Expensive.*

Atlantis. Those who associate Stouffer with frozen dinners will be happily surprised by the tasteful surroundings, the subdued atmosphere, and the sophisticated French menu. The waiters, even the busboys, are formally attired and very helpful. For an appetizer, try the warm duck salad. For entrees, the specialties are rack of lamb blackened with Cajun spices and served with an avocado cream sauce and swordfish grilled to perfection (though you may want to tell them to remove the port-wine sauce). The rich desserts border on divinity. *Stouffer Resort, 6677 Harbor Dr., Orlando, tel. 407/351–5555. Jackets required. Reservations recommended. AE, CB, DC, MC, V. Expensive.*

★   **Dux.** In the Peabody Hotel's gourmet restaurant, some creations are innovative, such as the grilled quail with poached quail eggs, served with wild rice in a carrot terrine nest. Others are a trifle self-conscious, like the avocado with sautéed salmon, artichoke chips, and champagne caviar sauce. For an entree, consider the baked Florida lobster with chanterelle mushrooms, spinach, and champagne sauce. The selection of California wines is outstanding. *Peabody Hotel, 9801 International Dr., Orlando, tel. 407/352–4000. Jacket required. Reservations strongly recommended. AE, CB, DC, MC, V. Expensive.*

La Coquina. This is a hotel restaurant with an emphasis on seafood and serious sauces. One popular meat specialty is loin of lamb with eggplant and goat cheese in grape leaves, served with grilled *polenta* (Italian-style cooked cornmeal). Best bet here is Sunday brunch—a cornucopia of fruits, vegetables, pastries, pâtés, smoked fish, and a number of dishes cooked before your eyes. The $27 brunch is served with Domaine Chandon champagne; the $52 brunch, with all the Dom Perignon champagne you can consume. If you're hungry and thirsty enough, you just might be able to put them out of business. *Hyatt Regency at Grand Cypress Resort, tel. 407/239–1234. Jackets required. Reservations suggested. AE, CB, DC, MC, V. Expensive.*

Indian **Darbar.** This lavishly decorated dining room features northern Indian cuisine. In addition to curries and pilafs, Darbar specializes in tandoori cooking—traditional Indian baking in a clay oven. Meats and vegetables are marinated in special sauces overnight and cooked to perfection. If you're unfamiliar with Indian cuisine, this is a good place to begin. Best bet is the tandoori dinner for two, with different types of lamb and chicken. *7600 Dr. Phillips Blvd., Orlando, tel. 407/345–8128. Dress: casual. Reservations advised on weekends. AE, DC, MC, V. Moderate. To get there, take Sand Lake Blvd. (Exit 29 of I–4) and head west to the Marketplace Shopping Center (just after the second stoplight). The restaurant is in the shopping center.*

Italian **Christini's.** For traditional Italian cuisine, this is Orlando's finest. The restaurant is not about to win any awards for decor, but the food couldn't be more fresh, and the service couldn't be more efficient. This is the kind of upscale Italian restaurant you might find in New York. The restaurant makes its own pastas daily and serves them with herbs, vegetables, and freshly grated Parmesan. Specialties include fresh fish; a fish soup with lobster, shrimp, and clams; and veal chops with fresh sage. *Intersection of Sand Lake Rd. and Dr. Phillips Blvd., in the Marketplace Shopping Center, tel. 407/345–8770. Jackets required. Reservations recommended. AE, CB, DC, MC, V. Expensive.*

★ **Cappriccio.** This is a smart-looking, California-chic Italian eatery, slickly decorated with granite and marble tiles. The menu features traditional and innovative pasta dishes such as spinach fettuccine with smoked salmon and mushrooms in a cream sauce. Also special are the exotic pizzas, cooked in old-fashioned wood-burning brick ovens. Try the *pizza ai cinque formaggi* (pizza made with sun-dried tomatoes, five cheeses, fresh herbs, and tons of garlic). It's a far cry from the Pizza Hut, so be prepared for deep-dish prices. *Peabody Hotel, 9801 International Dr., Orlando, tel. 407/352–4000. Dress: casual. Reservations recommended. AE, CB, DC, MC, V. Moderate.*

Japanese **Ran-Getsu.** The best Japanese food in town is served in this palatial setting. The atmosphere may seem a bit self-conscious—an American's idea of the Orient—but the food is fresh and carefully prepared. Sit at the curved, dragon's-tail-shaped sushi bar for the Matsu platter—an assortment of *nigiri-* and *maki*-style sushis—or, if you are with a group, sit Japanese-style at tables overlooking a carp-filled pond and decorative gardens. Specialties are sukiyaki and shabu-shabu, the latter thinly sliced beef in a boiling seasoned broth, served with vegetables and prepared at your table. If you feel more adventurous, try the deep-fried alligator tail. *8400 International Dr., Orlando, tel. 407/345–0044. Dress: casual. Reservations accepted. AE, DC, MC, V. Moderate.*

Kosher **Palm Terrace.** This is a Kosher restaurant supervised by Rabbi Jakobs of the Orthodox Union. Diners who are not guests at the Hyatt Orlando pay a fixed price of just under $30 (half-price half portions for children) for Shabbas meals. Meals must be prepaid on Fridays and reservations are required a half hour before candle lighting. Kosher breakfast and lunch items are available next door at the **Marketplace Deli** from 6 AM to midnight. (The Hyatt also offers a schul, with services held twice daily.) *Hyatt Orlando, 6375 Irlo Bronson Memorial Hwy., Kissimmee, tel. 407/396–1234. Dress: informal. Reservations required. AE, CB, DC, MC, V. Moderate.*

Seafood **Hemingway's.** Located by the pool at the Hyatt Regency Grand Cypress, this restaurant serves up all sorts of sea creatures from conch, scallops, and squid to grouper, pompano, and monkfish. In addition to the regular menu, Hemingway's also has what is called a "Cuisine Naturelle" menu, featuring dishes that are low in fat, calories, sodium, and cholesterol—recipes that are approved by the American Heart Association and Weight Watchers. What more could you want, other than a big hot-fudge sundae for dessert? *Hyatt Regency Grand Cypress Resort, tel. 407/239–1234. Dress: casual. Reservations suggested. AE, CB, DC, MC, V. Moderate–Expensive.*

24 Hours **Beeline Diner.** This is a slick 1950s-style diner that's always open. It is in the Peabody Hotel, so it's not exactly cheap, but the salads, sandwiches, and griddle foods are tops. Though very busy at times, it can be fun for breakfast or a late-night snack. And for just a little silver you get to play a lot of old tunes on the jukebox. *Peabody Hotel, 9801 International Dr., Orlando, tel. 407/352–4000. Dress: casual. Reservations not necessary. AE, CB, DC, MC, V. Moderate.*

Epcot Center

World Showcase offers some of the finest dining to be found not only in Walt Disney World but in the entire Orlando area. The problem is that the restaurants are often very crowded and difficult to book. Many of them are operated by the same people who own internationally famous restaurants in their home countries. The top-of-the-line places, such as those in the French, Italian, and Japanese pavilions, can be expensive, but they are not as pricey as comparable restaurants in large, cosmopolitan cities such as Paris or New York. One good thing about Epcot's restaurants, besides the food, is that most of them have limited-selection children's menus with dramatically lower prices, so bringing the kids along to dinner won't break the bank.

Visitors are not expected to go all the way back to their hotels to change and clean up and then return for dinner, so casual dress is not only permitted but expected in all of the restaurants, even the finest.

If you want to eat in one of the more popular restaurants, it will be much easier to get a reservation for lunch than for dinner. It won't be quite the same experience, but it will be cheaper. Another way to get a table is to have lunch before noon, and dinner before 6 PM or after 8 PM.

Both lunch and dinner reservations are strongly recommended at any of the finer restaurants in Epcot, and even at some of the not-so-fine. Making them, particularly in a busy season, can be time consuming. Reservations are accepted on a first-come, first-served basis for both lunch and dinner. Unless you are staying at one of the Disney World hotels, you cannot reserve in advance of the day on which you wish to eat, and you can't book by phone. Instead, you must head for Earth Station at the base of Spaceship Earth as soon as you get to Epcot. In Earth Station you will find a bank of computer screens called WorldKey Information. This is where things can get ugly. You need to stand in line to get to one of these screens and place the reservation, and the lines form very early. On busy days, most of the top restaurants are filled within an hour of Epcot's official opening time, so if you want to be sure of getting a reservation, you may have to line up well ahead of Epcot's actual opening time (which, as you may remember, may be as much as an hour ahead of the *published* opening time). Then, once you're through the gate, make a mad dash for the WorldKey computer terminals. If there is a long line when you get to Earth Station, remember that on the far side of Future World, just before the bridge to World Showcase, is an outdoor kiosk with five WorldKey terminals that few people notice. There is also another WorldKey kiosk on the far side of the Port of Entry gift shop, near the boat dock for the water taxi to Morocco. Having made the reservations, you can wipe the beads of sweat from your brow and begin to enjoy your day at Epcot.

It is also possible to reserve in person at a restaurant on the day you want to dine. The problem is that most restaurants don't open until 10 or 11 AM, and by then, in a busy season, all tables will be gone. Of course, it's always worth stopping by during the day and hoping someone has just cancelled.

If you are a guest at a Disney-owned hotel or at one of the Walt Disney World Hotel Plaza hotels, you can avoid the battle of the WorldKey by booking a table by phone (tel. 407/828–4000). Remember that if you are staying at one of these resorts you cannot make a same-day reservation by phone, but must book either one or two days in advance between noon and 9 PM. When making reservations, you'll be asked your name, resort, and room number. The restaurant will ask to see your resort identification card, so don't do something silly like leave it in your hotel room.

No matter how you book, try to show up at the restaurant a bit early to be sure of getting your table. You can pay with American Express, MasterCard, Visa, and, of course, cash. If you're a guest of an on-site hotel—both those owned by Disney and those that are not—you can charge the tab to your room.

British **Rose and Crown.** This is a very popular, friendly, British pub where visitors and Disney employees come at the end of the day to knock off a pint of crisp Bass Ale or blood-thickening Guinness Stout with a few morsels of Stilton cheese. "Wenches" serve up simple pub fare, such as steak-and-kidney pie, beef tenderloin, and fish and chips. The Rose and Crown sits on the shore of the lagoon, so on warm days it's nice to lunch on the patio at the water's edge and enjoy the soft breeze. Dark wood floors, pub chairs, and brass lamps create the warmest, most homey atmosphere in Epcot. The place is so friendly and comfortable that people come just to relax at the bar and chat with anyone who is around. The food is relatively inexpensive, especially at lunch, and the terrace has a great view of Illumi-Nations, so all things considered, it's one of the best finds in Epcot. Lunch and dinner entrees range between $6.25 and $16.95. *Moderate.*

French **Bistro de Paris.** Located on the second floor of the French pavilion, above Chefs de France (*see* below), this is a relatively quiet and charming spot for lunch or dinner. The Bistro specializes in regional cooking from southern France. A favorite is steamed filet of fresh grouper with tomato, mushrooms, fresh herbs, and white wine sauce, served with a rice pilaf. The wines are moderately priced and available by the glass. Lunch entrees $8.25–$14.25, dinner entrees $11.25–$18.95. *Expensive.*

Chefs de France. Three of France's most famous culinary artists came together to create this French restaurant. The most renowned of the three, Paul Bocuse, operates one restaurant north of Lyon and two in Tokyo, and has published several famous books on French cuisine. Another, Gaston Lenôtre, has gained eminence for his pastries and ice creams. The third of this culinary triumvirate, Roger Vergée, operates one of France's most highly touted restaurants, near Cannes. The three don't actually prepare each meal, but they were the ones who created the menu and carefully trained the chefs, and they look in frequently to make sure it's all up to snuff. Some of the most popular classic dishes are roast duck with prunes and wine sauce; beef filet with fresh ground pepper, raisins, and Armagnac sauce; and filet of grouper topped with salmon-vegetable mousse and baked in puff pastry. Lunch entrees $5.50–$11.25, dinner entrees $11.95–$18.25. *Expensive.*

German **Biergarten.** This popular spot boasts Oktoberfest 365 days a year. Visitors sit at long communal tables and are served by waitresses in typical Bavarian garb. The cheerful—some would say raucous—atmosphere is what one would expect from a place where performers yodel, sing, and dance to the rhythms of an oompah band. The crowd, pounding pitchers of beer or wine while consuming hot pretzels and hearty German fare, is usually pretty active when audience participation is called for, and just as active when it is not. Lunch and dinner entrees range between $6.50 and $16.95. *Moderate.*

Italian **L'Originale Alfredo di Roma Ristorante.** This is a World
★ Showcase hot spot with the most dynamic atmosphere and some of the finest food in Disney World. During dinner waiters skip around singing Italian songs and bellowing arias. At lunch you don't get the musical show, but the Italian waiters are usually entertaining enough to be a side show by themselves. If you are a pasta fan, this is the place for you. The restaurant is named for the same man who invented the now-classic fettuccine Alfredo, a pasta served with a sauce of cream, butter, and loads of freshly grated Parmesan cheese. It was this outstanding dish that made Alfredo de Lelio famous when he opened his original L'Originale Alfredo di Roma in 1914. Today it is operated by his grandson. Other than pasta, you should try *lo chef consiglia* (the Chef's Selection), which consists of an appetizer of spaghetti or fettuccine, a mixed green salad, and a chicken or veal entree. The most popular veal dish is *piccata di vitello*—veal thinly sliced and pan-fried with lemon and white wine. Lunch entrees $6.75–$16.95, dinner entrees $10.25–$22.95. *Expensive.*

Japanese **Mitsukoshi.** This isn't just a restaurant, it's a complex of dining
★ areas on the second floor above the Mitsukoski Department

Store. Each of the five dining rooms (on your left as you enter) has four tables, which seat eight and are equipped with a grill on which chefs prepare meats and fish with acrobatic precision. It's an American's idea of the real Japan, but fun nonetheless, especially if you are with a large group. Smaller parties may prefer going to the Tempura Kiku dining room on the right and sampling the tempura shrimp or thinly sliced Kabuki beef while sipping hot sake and enjoying a great view of the lagoon and Spaceship Earth. Lunch entrees $6.75–$9.50, dinner entrees $11.95–$18.50. *Moderate.*

Mexican **San Angel Inn.** The lush, tropical surrounding—cool, dark, almost surreal—makes this perhaps the most exotic restaurant in Disney World. The ambience is at once romantic and lively. Tables are candlelit, but close together, and the restaurant is open to the "sky" in the inside of the pavilion, where folk singers perform and musicians play guitars or xylophones. The best seats are along the outer edge of the restaurant, opposite the entrance, directly above the "river," with its boats streaming by, and below the Aztec pyramid, with its soft, fiery light evoking a sense of the distant past. The air-conditioning is often on high, so you may want to bring a light sweater. One of the specialties is *Langosta Baja California*—Baja lobster meat sauteed with tomatoes, onions, olives, Mexican peppers, and white wine, and baked in its shell—not exactly the sort of dish that comes to mind when you think of Mexican food. Try the margaritas, and, for dessert, don't miss the chocolate Kahlua mousse pie. Lunch entrees $5.25–$12.50, dinner entrees $9.50–$19.95. *Moderate.*

Moroccan **Marrakesh.** Belly dancers and a three-piece Moroccan band set the mood in this exotic restaurant, where you may feel as though you have stumbled onto the set of *Casablanca*, or the African continent itself. The food is mildly spicy and relatively inexpensive. Try the national dish of Morocco, *couscous*, served with garden vegetables; or *bastila*, an appetizer of sweet and spicy pork between many layers of thin pastry, with almonds, saffron, and cinnamon. Lunch entrees $6.95–$10.95, dinner entrees, $7.50–$15.50. *Moderate.*

Norwegian **Restaurant Akershus.** Norway's tradition of seafood and cold-meat dishes is highlighted at the restaurant's *koldtbord*, or Norwegian buffet. Hosts and hostesses explain the dishes to guests and suggest which ones go together. It is traditional to make several trips to the *koldtbord*, so there is no need to shovel everything you see onto your plate at one time. The first trip is for appetizers, usually herring. On your next trip choose cold seafood items—try gravlaks, salmon cured with salt, sugar, and dill. Pick up cold salads and meats on your next trip, and then, on your fourth trip, you fill up with hot dishes, usually a choice of lamb, veal, and venison. Desserts are offered à la carte, including cloudberries, delicate, seasonal fruits that grow on the tundra. There are four dining rooms, seating 220 in an impressive copy of Oslo's famous Akershus Castle. Lunch entrees are under $9 and dinners are priced under $14. *Moderate.*

The Orlando Area

The following restaurants are in or near the city of Orlando and cater mostly to a local clientele.

American **The Bubble Room.** Some visitors will get a real kick out of this upbeat nostalgia-theme restaurant with its big-band era music and wacky, wall-to-wall decor from the 1930s, '40s, and '50s. Every inch of space is covered with bric-a-brac, framed movie stills, photographs, autographed headshots, and magazine covers of bygone luminaries. Not only is the place fun and crazy, but the food is pretty wild as well. The menu is a hodgepodge of the Bubble Room's own interpretations of recipes from around the world, from Asian to Cajun. Seafood is shipped daily from the Gulf Coast, and the specialty of the house, "The Eddie Fisherman," is a filet of local black grouper covered with a light nut-crumb topping and then poached in a brown paper bag. *1351 S. Orlando Ave. (on Rte. 17–92), Maitland, tel. 407/628–3331. Dress: very casual. Reservations recommended. AE, CB, DC, MC, V. Moderate.*

Continental **Chalet Suzanne.** If you like to drive or are returning from a day
★ at Cypress Gardens, consider making a dinner reservation at this award-winning family-owned country inn and restaurant. It has been expanded bit by quirky bit since it opened in the 1930s, and today it looks like a small Swiss village—right in the middle of Florida's orange belt. The restaurant itself is filled with a hodgepodge of furniture from all over the world. The place settings, china, glasses, chairs, even the tables are of different sizes, shapes, and origins. Strangely, however, it all works together as the expression of a single sensibility. For an appetizer, try broiled grapefruit. Recommended among the seven entrees are chicken Suzanne, shrimp curry, lobster Newburg, shad roe, and filet mignon. Crepes Suzanne are a good bet for dessert. The seven-course meals begin at $40. The wine list offers many excellent choices at reasonable prices. Guests may step into the cellar and taste some of the wines that are being featured that night. Because of its charm and originality, the Chalet Suzanne has earned praise from restaurant critics— and for good reason. This unlikely back road country inn should provide one of the most memorable dining experiences one can have in Orlando. *U.S. 27 north of Lake Wales, about 10 mi past Cypress Gardens turnoff, tel. 813/676–6011. Jackets requested. Reservations suggested. AE, CE, DC, MC, V. Expensive. Closed Mon. during summer.*

Park Plaza Gardens. This popular spot is a see-and-be-seen experience for the locals of beautiful old Winter Park. At lunch, the society grand dames enjoy fabulous salads and quiches among an assortment of local secretaries and yuppies on business lunches. In the evening, the area's well-heeled families come here to dine. The dinner menu emphasizes seafood and veal. For dessert, the baked Alaska is a must. During the day, the restaurant is a bright greenhouse filled with plants; at night it is candlelit and romantic. On Sunday there is a good champagne brunch at bargain prices. *319 Park Ave. S., Winter Park, tel. 407/645–2475. Jackets usually worn but not required. Reservations advised. AE, CB, DC, MC, V. Moderate.*

French **Coq au Vin.** The atmosphere here is Mobile Home Modern, but
★ the traditional French fare is first-class, and you can pride yourself on discovering a place few tourists know about but that is nearly always filled with a friendly Orlando clientele. Owners Louis Perrotte (the chef) and his wife Magdalena (the hostess), make a charming couple who give the place its warmth and homey personality. Their specialties are home-

made chicken liver pâté, fresh rainbow trout with champagne, and roast Long Island duck with green peppercorn sauce. For dessert, try the crème brûlée. *4800 S. Orange Ave., Orlando, tel. 407/851–6980. Dress: informal. Reservations suggested. AE, CB, DC, MC, V. Moderate.*

Mexican Villa las Palomas. The building itself is a relatively faithful re-creation, inside and out, of its parent restaurant, the San Angel Inn, built in 1692 near Mexico City. It is a shame that the restaurant's architectural charm is lost along a street lined with gas stations and shopping malls, but on entering you feel as though you have crossed the border and stepped into an elegant Mexican inn. The menu includes traditional fare such as burritos and enchiladas, but it would be a shame not to try more ambitious dishes such as *Mole poblano*, a roasted half chicken simmered in a sauce of more than 20 Mexican spices. The food can be a bit heavy, so you may want to stick with seafood. The margaritas are first-class. Mexican guitarists will sing requests for you, and on weekends there is a 10-piece mariachi band. *3552 E. Colonial Dr., Orlando, tel. 407/894–2610. Dress: casual. Reservations accepted. AE, CB, DC, MC, V. Moderate.*

Pizza Rossi's. This is a local pizza joint—a garlic-bread-pepperoni-pizza-and-a-pitcher-of-Bud-or-rootbeer type of spot. The food is not about to win any awards, but Rossi's is a good escape from the tourist/hotel scene, and the price is *so* right. *5919 S. Orange Blossom Trail, Orlando, tel. 407/855–5755. Dress: very informal. AE, MC, V. Inexpensive.*

Seafood South Seas. The only problem here is deciding on which of the 70 seafood dishes to order. Whatever you choose, it's likely to be fresh, for the kitchen is supplied by the restaurant's own fish market. The large, modern dining room gets no points for ambience, but the variety of fish is staggering and the prices are the best around. Sink your teeth into alligator or shark that won't bite back, crack open some lobster or oysters, butter up some catfish or snapper. Steak and burgers are also served, but that would be like ordering a quarter-pounder with cheese from Colonel Saunders. *3001 Curry Ford Rd., Orlando, tel. 407/898–8331. Dress: casual. Reservations not accepted. AE, MC, V. Moderate.*

Steak Cattle Ranch. If you're hungry and looking for a big, thick, juicy, down-home American steak, then steer for the Cattle Ranch. It's cheap, and, if you're insanely hungry, it's free. Just take "The 6-pound Challenge," in which you're allowed 75 minutes to eat an entire six-pound steak dinner, including salad, potato, and bread. If you can do it, you won't have to pay a dime. If you can't, it will cost you just over 30 bucks. There is absolutely nothing fancy about this cowboy cafeteria except the steaks that come off the burning orangewood fire. And you won't see another tourist for miles around. *6129 Old Winter Garden Rd., Orlando (2½ blocks west of Kirkman Rd.), tel. 407/298–7334. Dress: very informal. Reservations: don't bother. AE, MC, V. Inexpensive.*

24 Hours Skeeter's. After Orlando's nightclubs close, both old and young stagger over to this popular diner to sober up or to prolong the party over some fried eggs, hash browns, and pancakes. A fun diner with lots of local character, open around the clock. *1212*

Lee Rd., Orlando, tel. 407/298–7973. Dress: casual. No credit cards. Inexpensive.

8 Lodging

Introduction

To stay within Disney World or without—that is the question.

The law of inertia seems to keep most Disney World guests within its realm. And if you are coming to Orlando for only a few days and are interested solely in the Magic Kingdom, Epcot, and the other Disney attractions, the resorts on Disney property are the most convenient. But if you plan to visit other attractions, you should at least consider the alternatives.

Let's look at the pros and cons of staying in an on-site hotel. On the positive side, you won't need to drive, and transportation within Disney World will be free. None of the hotels are within the actual confines of the Magic Kingdom or Epcot, but transportation is usually quick and efficient. Staying on-site allows you to visit the parks in the early morning, to return to your hotel for some R&R when the park crowds are thickest, and to return to the parks in the evening when the lines are shortest.

If you have kids, they will be able to travel on their own and to stay out of trouble within Disney World. Rooms in the on-site resorts are large and can as a rule accommodate up to five persons (villas sleep six or seven). Built with families in mind, the rooms offer cable television with the Disney Channel and a channel providing the latest updates on special daily events.

The thrill—especially for younger children—of knowing you are actually living in Disney World may in itself be worth staying here. The hotels offer many of their own special events such as theme dinner shows and breakfasts at which Disney cartoon characters come to entertain the kids. You don't need to stay in these hotels to enjoy these special programs, but it's nice to have them only an elevator ride or a short walk away.

As a Disney guest, you get first rights to tee-off times at the busy golf courses and you are able to call in advance to make hard-to-get reservations at any of the fine restaurants in Epcot Center. Outsiders can make reservations only in person in the park on the day they wish to dine.

As an on-site guest, you also get an identification card that allows you to charge most meals and purchases at Disney World (except in the Magic Kingdom) to your room.

On the negative side, hotels with comparable facilities tend to cost more on Disney property than off. You may think that by staying at a Disney hotel you'll get discounts on multiple-day passports. This is little more than a promotional ploy—unless you consider a savings of a few dollars on hundreds of dollars worth of passports a significant discount. Whatever small savings you may realize will be undercut by the higher cost of staying in an on-site property.

Furthermore, Disney World, family vacationland that it is, is packed with children, and couples may prefer a more relaxed atmosphere in which to spend the night (of course some off-site properties are just as crowded). Large conventions can create a less than ideal environment for both families and couples. Of course, if complete peace and quiet are what you're after, you should be thinking of another vacation altogether.

It is true that to the cost of an off-site hotel must be added the expense of transportation to Disney World, but shuttle service is frequent, convenient, and—if your family is small—relatively cheap.

Reservations

All on-site accommodations may be booked through the Walt Disney World Central Reservations Office, Box 10100, Lake Buena Vista, FL 32830, tel. 407/W–DISNEY. Reservations must often be made several months in advance and sometimes, for the best rooms, during high season, a year in advance. There are always cancellations, of course, so it's worth trying even at the last minute. Keep in mind that Delta Airlines (tel. 800/221–1212) has many rooms allotted to it for its travel packages, so check with Delta, too. Visitors on a tight budget should be aware that many hotels (and attractions) offer discounts up to 40% from September to mid-December.

If the on-site resorts are full, Central Reservations will automatically try to book a place for you at one of the Walt Disney World Village Hotel Plaza hotels. Be sure to tell them exactly what you are looking for. You must give a deposit for your first night's stay within three weeks of making your reservation, and you can get a refund if you cancel at least five days before your scheduled stay.

Land packages, including admissions tickets, car rentals, and hotels either on or off Disney property, can be made through **Walt Disney Travel Co.** (1675 Buena Vista Dr., Lake Buena Vista, FL 32830, tel. 407/828–3232).

Land/air packages, with accommodations both on and off Disney property, can be booked through **Disney Reservation Service** (tel. 800/828–0228).

Ratings

The most highly recommended properties in each price category are indicated by a star★. Rates usually include the price of two children under 18.

Category	Cost*
Very Expensive	over $150
Expensive	$120–$150
Moderate	$65–$120
Inexpensive	under $65

*double room; add 9% for taxes

Disney-Owned Hotels

Visitors have a choice of staying at (1) hotels owned and operated by Disney, (2) hotels that are privately owned but that are located on Disney property, and (3) hotels in the Orlando area.

Let's look at the Disney-run hotels first. In brief, the **Contemporary** is the biggest and busiest resort—the one that is most crowded with children and conventioneers. Yet it is also the center of action, with the most entertainment, shops, and restaurants.

The **Polynesian Village** is the most popular, particularly with families and couples. It has a relaxed environment with low, tropical buildings and walking paths along the Seven Seas Lagoon. It can be difficult to find a place to be alone, however.

The charm of the **Grand Floridian** will survive the crowds. The waterfront location makes it particularly attractive.

The most relaxed and low-key of the hotels is the **Disney Inn.** It is the smallest, and, because it is between two golf courses, it is the quietest.

The **Caribbean Beach Resort** is the low-cost option for those guests who want the convenience of being on Disney property without the high prices (rooms start at $65 a night).

The **Resort Villas** are especially attractive for families or groups of two or more couples. There are four different types of villas in relatively isolated woodland settings.

Least formal are the completely equipped trailer and camp sites in the even more wooded **Fort Wilderness Campground Resort.**

Reservations sometimes become available at the last minute. For same-day reservations, phone each Disney property directly. For advance reservations call 407/W–DISNEY.

Contemporary Resort. The futuristic monorail runs right through the middle of this gigantic A-frame hotel, making visitors feel they have truly arrived in Tomorrowland. But once you're inside the space station of an atrium, visitors find themselves back to the present, in a rather impersonal, bustling world of restaurants, lounges, and shops. Only half of the hotel's rooms are here in this 15-story tower. They are the more expensive rooms because of their spectacular views—the higher up the better. Rooms in the front are at a premium because they look out toward the Magic Kingdom, and guests can watch the sun set and the fireworks explode over Cinderella Castle. Rooms on the back side have ringside seats for the Electrical Water Pageant and sunrise through the mists of Bay Lake.

The rest of the hotel's rooms are in the North and South Gardens. Tower rooms can be somewhat noisy at night—sounds rise through the crowded atrium—so if you're a light sleeper, stay in one of the quieter wings. The wings are less expensive, and overlook the hotel's pool and gardens; the best rooms overlook Bay Lake. Try to avoid rooms that look out over the parking lot, even though they may be described as having a view of the Magic Kingdom.

All the rooms in the hotel have a small terrace and most of them have two queen-size beds and a small bed for one additional person to sleep—less than comfortably. You can request a room with a king-size bed and double sofa bed. Every room has a large bathroom with double sinks, tub, and shower.

The hotel has many recreational facilities including tennis courts available at hourly rates, two swimming pools, and many water sports at its own lake marina. There is also a health club with co-ed activities in the morning and separate hours for men and women during the day.

The 4th floor Grand Canyon Concourse in the tower has numerous shops selling gifts, clothing, and books. For Continental cuisine and candlelight consider the leisurely Gulf Coast Room. The fast-paced Top of the World restaurant offers nightly Broadway revues and live jazz. (Jackets required at both restaurants.) Kids will be happy to disappear into the Fiesta Fun Center, filled with every imaginable game room activity. They will also enjoy meeting the Disney characters who show up for breakfast at the Terrace Cafe.

The Contemporary is a very busy place filled with conventions and crowds but it does have many conveniences. The monorail can take you to the Polynesian Hotel, the Magic Kingdom, and Epcot; and a motor launch can take you directly to Discovery Island and Fort Wilderness/River Country. The boat leaves from the marina behind the hotel about every 20 minutes. (Admission: $12 adults, $8 children 3–9.) *WDW Central Reservations, Box 10100, Lake Buena Vista 32830, tel. 407/W–DISNEY or 824–1000 for same-day reservations. 1,052 rooms. AE, MC, V. Expensive–Very Expensive.*

Polynesian Village Resort. You are supposed to get the feeling that you are on a tropical island when you come here, so everything at the recently redecorated Poly, as it's called, has a South Pacific slant to it. The focal point of the resort is the Great Ceremonial House, where visitors check in. The atrium sets the tone with its lush tropical atmosphere complete with volcanic rock fountains, blooming orchids, coconut palms, and the constant rush of running water—the whole bit. You might think you were at a resort in Fiji if you didn't notice all the kids running around wearing Mickey Mouse caps.

Stretching from the main building are 11 two- and three-story "longhouses," each of which carries the name of some exotic Pacific Island. All rooms offer two queen-size beds and a smaller sleeper sofa, and accommodate up to five people. Except for some second-floor rooms, all have a balcony or patio.

If you don't like to walk too much and want to be near the main building with its shops and entertainment, request a room in the Bora Bora or Maui longhouses. For the best view of the Magic Kingdom and the Seven Seas Lagoon with its sandy, palm-trimmed beaches, stay in the Samoa, Moorea, or Tonga.

The least expensive rooms look out at the other buildings, the monorail, and the parking lot across the street. Slightly more expensive are the garden-and-pool-view rooms. Rooms overlooking the lagoon are the priciest, but they are also the most peaceful, and include a host of upgraded amenities and services that make them among the most sought after in Disney World. They, too, have a perfect view of the Electrical Water Pageant. Recreational activities center around the hotel's large sandy beach and marina, where you can rent boats for sailing, waterskiing, and fishing. If you can pull together a group of eight, you can even rent an outrigger canoe. The two swimming pools can be overrun by children; you may want to go to the beach for a dip instead. One pool is free-form and wonderfully landscaped with rocks and caverns at one end.

The Polynesian Village Resort is the most popular of all Disney-owned resorts, particularly among families and honeymooners. Some 60% of the guests have been here before, so the resort must be doing something right. *WDW Central Reservations, Box 10100, Lake Buena Vista 32830, tel. 407/W–DISNEY or 824–2000 for same-day reservations. 855 rooms. AE, MC, V. Expensive–Very Expensive.*

★ **Disney Inn.** This is the smallest and quietest of the Disney hotels. At one time, it was called the Golf Resort and non-golfers stayed away. Others were turned off by the fact that the monorail did not stop here. The problem was easily solved by dropping the "Golf" and replacing it with the biggest name in tourism this side of Mecca, and changing "Resort" to "Inn" to signal the away-from-it-all quality of a country hostelry.

The truth is that while the resort sits between two world-class golf courses and a number of golfers *do* like to stay here, the place is a great spot for couples—with or without family in tow —especially if they want to escape the more frenzied activity found at the other resorts. Rooms at the Disney Inn are slightly larger than most rooms at the other resorts. Up to five persons can sleep in two queen-size beds and a comfortable sleeper sofa. The most expensive rooms overlook the pool. If you book a room on the first floor, you can walk directly from your room to the pool; however, these rooms can be noisy at times. Less expensive rooms with views of the gardens or, better yet, the fairways are equally pleasant and quieter.

As you can guess, the recreation here focuses mostly on driving and putting skills. There are three first-rate 18-hole golf courses and a 9-hole beginner's course. These golf facilities are open to the public, but Disney guests are accommodated first. *WDW Central Reservations, Box 10100, Lake Buena Vista 32830, tel. 407/W–DISNEY or 824–2200 for same-day reservations. 288 rooms. AE, MC, V. Expensive.*

★ **The Grand Floridian.** If you are looking for old-fashioned character, style, charm, and luxury, but also want all the conveniences of a modern hotel, the Grand Floridian Beach Resort is for you. At first glance you may think that Disney found this gilded-age masterpiece in Palm Beach or some other turn-of-the-century coastal hotspot and transported it to the shores of the Seven Seas Lagoon. But, no, the resort opened August 1, 1988. The gabled red roofing, brick chimneys, and long rambling verandahs were all built with loving attention to detail. Inside, crystal chandeliers, stained-glass domes, and ornate latticework on balconies and aviaries create the feeling of an earlier, less frenetic age. The rooms are somewhat more modern, but subdued and tasteful, with light-wood furniture and soft colors.

The hotel has five bustling restaurants, two lounges, and merchandise shops featuring turn-of-the-century items.

As you may expect from a beach resort, there are all sorts of water sports at the marina and enclosed boardwalk pier. Facilities include a health club, an outdoor pool and a spa. The Grand Floridian also has its own monorail stop that links it to the Transportation and Ticket Center and the Magic Kingdom. Even the resort's monorail station carries off the elegant Victorian theme. *WDW Central Reservations, 10100 Lake Buena Vista 32830, tel. 407/W–DISNEY. 652 standard rooms; 167 smaller "attic" chambers; 69 concierge rooms; 12 suites. AE, MC, V. Expensive–Very Expensive.*

The Caribbean Beach Resort. Like the Polynesian Village Resort, the Caribbean Beach Resort is made up of villages—Aruba, Barbados, Jamaica, Martinique, and Trinidad—all two-story buildings on a 42-acre tropical lake. Each village has its own swimming pool, laundry facility, and stretch of white-sand beach. Bridges over the lake connect the mainland with Parrot Cay, a one-acre island featuring footpaths, bike paths, and children's play areas. There is a 500-seat food court and an adjoining 200-seat lounge. Check-in is at the Custom House, off Buena Vista Drive. *WDW Central Reservations, 10100 Lake Buena Vista 32830, tel. 407/W–DISNEY or 407/934–3400. 1,200 one-bedroom units. AE, MC, V. Moderate.*

The Resort Villas

There are a few good reasons why you may prefer the Resort Villas to the resort hotels.

• You are visiting Disney with your family or with other couples and you want to stay together and avoid the expense of separate rooms.
• You enjoy the convenience of having your own kitchen and would like to save money by preparing some of your own meals.
• You don't like big, busy hotels but you appreciate the amenities of a resort.

There are five types of villas, each with its own character and ambience. Though they are not quite as plush as rooms in the resort hotels, they are more spacious. Since the villas are not on the monorail, transportation to the parks can be slow, and to get around within the village you may want to use your car or a rented bike or golf cart. On the positive side, you have immediate access to great golf, great fishing, shopping, and an active nightlife. Check-in for resort villas is at the entrance to Disney Village Resort. *WDW Central Reservations, 10100 Lake Buena Vista 32830, tel. 407/W–DISNEY or 827–1100 for same-day reservations.*

The Vacation Villas They were originally built in 1971, but—thank goodness—were refurbished in 1986. Each unit has complete living facilities with equipped kitchens and either one or two bedrooms. The one-bedroom villas have a king-size bed in one room and a queen-size sofa bed in the living room (accommodating up to four). The two-bedroom units (accommodating up to six) have either a king-size bed or two twins in each bedroom, and a living-room sofa bed. There are two outdoor pools at the Vacation Villas. *139 one-bedroom units, 87 two-bedroom units. AE, MC, V. Expensive–Very Expensive.*

Club Suite Villas. These are the smallest and the least memorable of the villas—and also the least expensive. Built of cedar, they have one bedroom, a sofa bed, a wet bar, but no kitchens—the only villas that don't. Their size and ambience reflect the needs of the business people attending meetings at the nearby WDW Conference Center. Facilities include two outdoor pools, a small game room, a playground, and boat rentals. *61 units. Expensive.*

Two-Bedroom Villas. These villas are built of cedar, like those at Club Suite, but they are more tastefully decorated and very spacious. All have two bedrooms and a full loft, accommodating up to six. They were formerly known as the Fairway Villas because the property is surrounded by several fairways of the Lake Buena Vista Golf Course. Guests may use pools at the Villa Recreation Center or Walt Disney World Village Clubhouse. *64 units. Expensive–Very Expensive.*

Three-Bedroom Villas. If you really want to get away from it all, this is the place to stay. Isolated within a peaceful, heavily wooded area, these curious "treehouse" villas stand on stilts. You won't exactly feel like Tarzan and Jane in these bungalows, but you may hear some howls late at night. Predictably, this out-of-the-way little forest retreat is popular among young couples. All treehouses accommodate six and have two bedrooms with queen-size beds and a third bedroom with a double bed, kitchen and breakfast bar, living room, and two bathrooms. The third bedroom is on a lower level. There is also a utility room with washer/dryer. Guests can use nearby pools at the Villa Recreation Center or Walt Disney World Village Clubhouse. *60 units. Expensive–Very Expensive.*

Fort Wilderness. If you want to rough it, stay here among 730 acres of woodland, streams, small lakes, and plenty of water activities along the southeastern edge of Bay Lake, at the northern edge of Disney World property. You can rent a 42-foot-long trailer (accommodating up to six) or a 35-foot trailer (accommodating up to four). Both types have one bedroom, a bath, a full kitchen, air-conditioning, heat, and daily housekeeping services. The trailer sites are spread over 80 forested acres.

For those who are more serious about getting in touch with the great outdoors, there are campsites spread across 21 areas. Some are for visitors' own trailers, complete with electrical outlets, outdoor charcoal grills, private picnic tables, water, and waste disposal. Full maid service is available. There are also tent sites with water and electricity but not sewage. The most expensive sites (100 through 700) are nearest the lake. The least expensive (1600 through 1900) are far from the lake in denser vegetation. If there's bargain lodging at WDW, this is it. Each site accommodates up to 10 people. The campground has its own beach, swimming pools, volleyball and tennis courts, and all sorts of boats for rent.

Fort Wilderness also offers a huge water playground called River Country, with raft rides, rope swings, a winding water slide, and a huge heated pool. Nearby, in the middle of Bay Lake, is Discovery Island, a nature preserve with more than 60 species of animals and rare birds amidst hundreds of varieties of exotic flowers, plants, and trees. You can get a boat to the island from Fort Wilderness. *WDW Central Reservations, Box 10100, Lake Buena Vista 32830, tel. 407/W–DISNEY, or same-day reservations 407/824–2900. Trailers, moderate; campsites, inexpensive.*

Lake Buena Vista Village

The formal name of this area is Walt Disney World Village Hotel Plaza at Lake Buena Vista, but most people refer to it simply as Hotel Plaza. Next to the resorts that are actually Disney-owned, these seven hotels are the most popular among visitors to Walt Disney World. This is because the properties publicize themselves as "official Walt Disney World hotels" and offer many of the same benefits. Many people believe these hotels are owned by Disney. Not true. They were invited to establish themselves on Disney property and they pay for the privilege. Disney does keep a close eye on them, however, to ensure that they maintain certain standards.

Because these hotels are on Disney property there is a premium on rooms and rates are somewhat inflated compared to what you can find off Disney property. Many Disney fans believe, however, that the benefits of staying in these hotels make it worthwhile. You decide.

• You can avoid box-office lines at Magic Kingdom and Epcot by buying tickets at your hotel. However, you can also send for these tickets before leaving home or purchase them at the airport. For a three-day passport, you get less than a 2% discount—a savings of only $1.
• You can make telephone reservations for restaurants and dinner shows in Disney World in advance of the general public.
• You can use the tennis and golf facilities at Lake Buena Vista Village.
• The Buena Vista hotels are all part of an attractively landscaped complex. Each has its own restaurants and lounges, and all are within walking distance of the popular Walt Disney World Shopping Village, a pleasant outdoor mall filled with gift shops and restaurants.
• Hotel Plaza hotels are convenient. Direct bus service is available to Epcot Center; to get to the Magic Kingdom, you get a direct bus to the TTC, then change for the monorail or ferry. So if half the family wants to spend the afternoon in one of the parks and the other half wants to go back to the hotel swimming pool, it's easy.

You can call each hotel's toll-free number for reservations, or you can book rooms at any of them through the **Walt Disney World Central Reservations Office** (CRO), Box 10100, Lake Buena Vista, FL 32830 tel. 407/W–DISNEY. Delta Airline offers reservations at these hotels for discount prices in their package deals.

To reach Lake Buena Vista Village, take I–4 west to the exit for Rte. 535, clearly marked Walt Disney World Village, Lake Buena Vista. Turn right, and at the first stoplight take a left into the Village. You will be on Hotel Plaza Blvd. The resort lines both sides of the street.

Buena Vista Palace. This is the largest of the Lake Buena Vista hotels, with one of its towers soaring 27 stories high. When you enter its lobby, the hotel seems smaller and quieter than its bold, modern exterior and sprawling parking lots might suggest. Don't be fooled. You have entered on the third floor; when you head down to the ground level, you'll see just how large this place truly is. Facilities include a health club, swimming pools, four tennis courts, a beauty salon, a game room, two gift shops, and a host of bars and restaurants. *The Outback*, an Australian-themed restaurant, serves steaks, lobsters, and 99 varieties of beer. Next door is a lively nightclub called *Laughing Kookaburra*. *Top of the Palace Lounge*, on the top floor, is a good perch for watching the sun set and Epcot Center's nightly bath in colored lights and lasers. Also on the top floor is the formal

Arthur's 27 restaurant, where a seven-course Continental meal costs about $55 per person.

Rooms are unmemorable but adequate, each with its own small patio and a push-button Mickey Mouse telephone. Rooms on the upper floors are more expensive; the best ones look out toward Epcot. Ask for a room in the main tower to avoid the late-night noise that reverberates through the atrium from the nightclub. *1900 Lake Buena Vista Dr., Lake Buena Vista 32830, tel. 407/827-2727 or 800/327-2990. 841 rooms. AE, CB, DC, MC, V. Expensive-Very Expensive.*

Grosvenor Resort. This attractive hotel is probably the best deal in the neighborhood, with a wealth of facilities and comfortable rooms for a fair price. The former Americana Dutch Resort, it has been completely refurbished in British colonial-style. Public areas are spacious, with high molded ceilings and columns, warm cheerful colors, and plenty of natural light. *Baskerville*'s serves Continental fare and Sherlock Holmes memorabilia. A homey little pub called *Moriarity*'s has live entertainment.

Recreational facilities are geared toward the active life and include two heated pools, two lighted tennis courts, racquetball, shuffleboard, basketball, and volleyball courts, a children's playground, and a game room. Rooms are average in size, but colorfully decorated, with a refrigerator/bar and a videocassette player. In the lobby you can rent movies for the VCR or cameras to make your own videos. *1850 Hotel Plaza Blvd., Lake Buena Vista 32830, tel. 407/828-4444 or 800/624-4109. 614 rooms. AE, CB, DC, MC, V. Moderate-Expensive.*

★ **Hilton at Walt Disney World Village.** The Hilton is generally considered the top hotel in the Village. It is also one of the most expensive. In contrast to the unimpressive facade, interiors are richly decorated with brass and glass, and softened with tasteful carpets. Guest rooms sparkle. Rooms are not huge, but they are cozy and contemporary, with high-tech amenities. All are the same size, with a king-size bed, two double beds, or two queen-size beds. The most expensive rooms have views of the Shopping Village and lake. Also desirable are rooms overlooking the pool. Although all rooms are the same size, they vary dramatically in price by location and floor, as well as by season. Keep in mind that if you book a room at the lowest rate—on a lower floor with a mediocre view—the check-in clerk can assign you to a better room if one is available, at an extra charge of $30.

The Hilton provides a service that many parents will consider indispensable—a Youth Hotel for children 3–12. It has full-time supervisors for its playroom, a large-screen television (with Disney Channel, of course), a six-bed dormitory, and scheduled meals. The Youth Hotel is open daily from 4 PM to midnight. The cost is $4 an hour.

Other facilities include two swimming pools, a health club, two lighted tennis courts, several outdoor and indoor bars and restaurants, including the popular *American Vineyards*, serving New American cuisine. *1751 Hotel Plaza Blvd., Lake Buena Vista 32830, tel. 407/827-4000 or 800/445-8667. 814 rooms. AE, MC, V. Expensive-Very Expensive.*

Howard Johnson, Lake Buena Vista. This is not the handsomest hotel on the block, but it is one of the most reasonably priced. Though somewhat charmless, with a white formica lobby and a lackluster 14-story atrium, the hotel is popular with young couples and senior citizens. There are two heated pools, a kiddie pool, a game room, and an upgraded Howard Johnson's restaurant that's open 24 hours. *1805 Hotel Plaza Blvd., Lake Buena Vista 32830, tel. 407/828–8888 or 800/654–2000. 323 rooms. AE, CB, DC, MC, V. Moderate–Very Expensive.*

Pickett Suite Resort. Walt Disney World is certainly not one to fall behind the current trends in the hotel industry, so it is not surprising that the most recent addition to the Lake Buena Vista neighborhood would be an all-suite hotel. Suites consist of a comfortable living-room area and a separate bedroom with either two double beds or a king-size bed. With a sofa bed in the living room, a suite can accommodate up to six people, but certainly not all comfortably. The arrangement is convenient for small families who want to avoid the hassle of cots and the expense of two separate rooms. Each unit has a television in each room (including a small one in the bathroom!), a stocked refrigerator, a wet bar, a coffeemaker, and, on request, a microwave oven. The hotel attracts a quiet family crowd and few of the noisy conventioneers you can expect to find at larger, splashier properties. Facilities include a whirlpool spa, heated pools, two tennis courts, a game room, and a children's play area. The terrace restaurant and bar are fine for the complimentary buffet breakfasts but you will probably want to drink and dine elsewhere. *2305 Hotel Plaza Blvd., Lake Buena Vista 32830, tel. 407/934–1000 or 800/742–5388. 229 units. AE, CB, DC, MC, V. Expensive–Very Expensive.*

Royal Plaza. From the lobby, this hotel seems a bit dated in comparison to the slick, modern hotels in the neighborhood. But the extremely casual, lively atmosphere makes it quite popular among families with young kids and teenagers. Rooms are generous in size, the best ones overlooking the pool. If you have any interest in sleeping late or napping in the afternoon, make sure your room isn't too close to the ground floor. The hotel has several restaurants and bars, a few shops, a hair salon, four lighted tennis courts, sauna, pool, and putting green. The flashy disco-nightclub called *The Giraffe* is open later than late. *La Cantina* may be the only piano bar you'll ever find with a 2-for-1 happy hour from midnight until closing time (3 AM), seven nights a week. *1905 Hotel Plaza Blvd., Lake Buena Vista 32830, tel. 407/828–2828 or 800/248–7890. 396 rooms. AE, CB, DC, MC, V. Expensive–Very Expensive.*

Viscount Hotel. There is nothing particularly notable about this hotel except that its popular *Top-of-the-Tower* nightclub, on the 18th floor, features live, upbeat guitar music, and enjoys a stellar view of Walt Disney World. The hotel was recently refurbished, so the lobby and rooms are stylishly decorated, but other than having minibars, the rooms are unexceptional. The pool, playground, and game room are popular with kids. *2000 Hotel Plaza Blvd., Lake Buena Vista 32830, tel. 407/828–2424, in FL 800/423–1022, outside FL 800/255–3050. 325 rooms. AE, CB, DC, MC, V. Expensive.*

Buena Vista Palace, **1**
Casa Rosa Inn, **21**
Cedar Lakeside Inn, **22**
Chalet Suzanne, **28**
Embassy Suites, **8**
Enclave Suites, **9**
Grand Cypress Resort, **17**
Grosvenor Resort, **2**
Hilton, **3**
Howard Johnson Lake Buena Vista, **4**
Hyatt Orlando, **16**
Marriott, **18**
Orlando Heritage Inn, **10**
Park Plaza, **27**
Park Suite, **11**
Peabody Orlando, **12**
Pickett Suite Resort, **5**
Raddison Inn, **13**
Raddison Inn Maingate, **23**
Ramada Resort Maingate East, **19**
Residence Inn, **24**
Royal Plaza, **6**
Sheraton Inn, **25**
Sonesta Village, **14**
Stouffer Orlando, **15**
Travelodge Golden Triangle, **26**
Viscount, **7**
Vistana, **20**

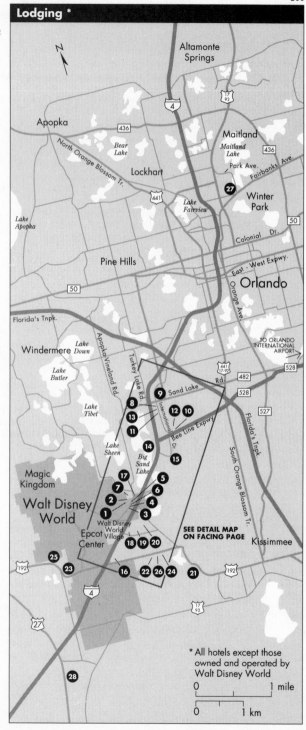

Lodging *

* All hotels except those owned and operated by Walt Disney World

0 ——————— 1 mile

0 ——————— 1 km

Lodging (detail) *

* All hotels except those owned and operated by Walt Disney World

The Orlando Area

The number of hotels, motels, and resorts in the Orlando area is simply astounding. Just about every American hotel chain has at least one hotel in the vicinity. One, Days Inn, has more than 6,500 guest rooms in 27 hotels within a 20-mile range of Disney World. That's a thick chain.

Since its birth as a tourist mecca, Orlando's hotel industry has grown continuously. New hotels of all sizes and varieties seem to open every day. In the early days of Disney World, the large hotels were limited primarily to Disney property, but more recently there has been a boom in huge resorts catering largely to business convention crowds. These have spread to International Drive. Whether you're staying in the inexpensive Kissimmee area (with its smaller hotels), along International Drive (with both large and small hotels), or anywhere around the Disney Maingate (around the northernmost entrance, just off I–4), nearly all hotels provide frequent transportation to and from Walt Disney World. What matters most is that you choose a hotel within your price range, where you can be comfortable.

International Drive

The International Drive area, referred to by locals as "The Drive" and formally labeled "Florida Center," is a main drag for all sorts of hotels, restaurants, and shopping malls. As you head north along the Drive, the hotels get cheaper, the restaurants turn into fast food joints, and malls translate into factory outlets. The southern end of the Drive is classier, but the northern end may be more congenial to your budget—particularly if all you need is a place to put your head at night.

You will be hard-pressed to find any structure around here older than you are, even if you are a teenager, since the area has been built up mostly in the last 10 years as an alternative to the Disney properties. For those not exclusively interested in Disney World, the Drive is a convenient point of departure for Orlando's countless other attractions. The Drive immediately parallels I–4 (at exits 28 and 29), so a few minutes' drive north puts you in downtown Orlando, while a few minutes south on I–4 puts you in Disney World.

International Drive showcases such local attractions as Sea World, Universal Studios, the labyrinth water-slide park, Wet 'n Wild, and many popular dinner shows. Many veteran Orlando visitors consider International Drive the territory's most comfortable home base, featuring some of the best hotels around.

Embassy Suites Hotel at Plaza International. The concept of the all-suite hotel has become very popular in the Orlando area, and the Embassy Suites, a chain hotel, was the first to offer it. All suites have both a bedroom and a full living room equipped with wet bar, refrigerator, desk, pull-out sofa, and two TVs. It is a comfortable and economical arrangement, somewhat less expensive than a single room in the top-notch hotels. Because the bedroom can be closed off, it is ideal for small families. The core of the hotel is a wide atrium. It is not nearly as large as the atrium at the Stouffer, but it is much cozier, with a relaxing lounge and pianist as its centerpiece. The hotel has an indoor and an outdoor pool, an exercise room with Jacuzzi and sauna, a steam room, and a game room, but none of the other recreational facilities of the larger hotels. *8250 Jamaica Ct., Orlando 32819, tel. 407/345–8250 or 800/327–9797. 246 rooms. AE, DC, MC, V. Moderate–Expensive.*

The Enclave Suites. This all-suite hotel is less a hotel than a condominium complex with three 10-story buildings surrounding an office, a restaurant, and a recreation area. The suites are like apartments, offering significantly more space than the other all-suite hotels. They contain full kitchens, living rooms, and small terraces. For about the same price as a room in a big, fancy hotel, you can have two bedrooms and all the amenities of home—with accommodations for up to six people. The arrangement is ideal for families or small groups of friends who want to get away from the hotel hustle. The single suites are great for couples. Weekly rates offer additional savings. Facilities include one indoor and two outdoor pools, a Jacuzzi and sauna, an exercise room, a lighted tennis court, a children's play area, and a restaurant called the *Enclave Beach Cafe* that is popular with local yuppies. *6165 Carrier Dr., Orlando 32819, tel. 407/351–1155 or 800/457–0077. 321 suites. AE, DC, MC, V. Moderate–Expensive.*

Orlando Heritage Inn. If you are looking for a simple, small hotel with reasonable rates but plenty of deliberate charm, the Heritage is the place to stay. Located next to the towering Peabody, this inn creates the atmosphere of Victorian-style Florida, complete with reproduction turn-of-the-century furnishings, rows of French windows and brass lamps, and a smattering of genuine 19th-century antiques. The guest rooms are decorated with a colonial accent—lace curtains on double French doors, folk art prints on the walls, and quilted bed covers. The hotel has a small saloon-type lounge, and there is a dinner theater in the large Victorian rotunda several nights a week. With the exception of a swimming pool, there are few facilities. The whole place has a kitschy quaintness, in contrast to the area's other hotels, and a staff that is strong on Southern hospitality. *9861 International Dr., Orlando 32819, tel. 407/352–0008, in FL 800/282–1890, or outside FL 800/ 447– 1890. 150 rooms. AE, DC, MC, V. Moderate.*

Park Suite. Park Suite is another all-suite hotel, similar to the Embassy Suites, but with a southern flavor. The lobby has an old-fashioned feeling to it, with marble floors and pillars, hanging lamps, and ceiling fans. When you step into the hotel's atrium you are struck by the faint, humid smell of the Deep South, which comes from its tropical gardens and mossy rock fountains. The suites are comfortable with all the amenities of the Embassy Suites, plus a microwave oven. The difference between these two all-suite hotels is that the Embassy is brassy modern while the Park, with its ceramic tile walkways and brick arches, exudes a sense of the past. Also, the rates at the Park are slightly lower. The Park has a restaurant and bar, exercise equipment, and a fancy indoor pool with whirlpool, steam room, and sauna. *8978 International Dr., Orlando 32819, tel. 407/352–1400 or 800/432–7272. 245 suites. AE, DC, MC, V. Moderate.*

Peabody Orlando. From afar, the Peabody looks like a high rise office building. Don't let its austere exterior scare you away! Once inside, you will discover a very impressive, handsomely designed hotel. If you ignore the soaring numbers in the elevators and the sweeping view from your room, you will never know you are in a skyscraping, 27-story hotel. The Peabody's lobby has rich marble floors and fountains, and the entire hotel is decorated with modern art, giving it much color and flair. The rooms with the best views face Disney World and a sea of orange trees that extends as far as the eye can see. If you want to be pampered, stay in the Peabody Clubs on the top three floors and enjoy special concierge service.

The hotel was built by the owners of the famous Peabody Hotel in Memphis, a landmark there since the 1920s. Following in the tradition of the Memphis Peabody, the Orlando hotel has as its symbol a mallard duck. Each morning at 11, ducks (yes, real ones) waddle in a parade down an elevator, through the lobby on a red carpet to spend the day around a marble fountain. They march back at 5 PM.

The Peabody has a pool, a health club, and four lighted tennis courts. There are also two fine restaurants, *Capriccio's* for Italian fare and *Dux* for Continental cuisine. There is also a 24-hour 1950s-style diner, the *Beeline*. Located across the street from the Orlando Convention/Civic Center, the hotel attracts concert performers from across the street and conventioneers. *9801 International Dr., Orlando. 32819, tel. 407/352–4000 or 800/262–6688. 891 rooms. AE, CB, DC, MC, V. Expensive–Very Expensive.*

Radisson Inn and Justus Aquatic Center. If you want to get in shape while visiting Orlando but want to avoid fancy resort prices, this is the place for you. Radisson is a big, modern, moderately priced hotel offering comfortable rooms (the best ones face the pool), but what makes it truly special are its outstanding athletic facilities. The hotel has a fine outdoor pool, but for those who are serious about swimming there is also an indoor Aquatic Center with an Olympic-size swimming and diving pool. The center was built for competitive swimming and diving events and has a high-tech Human Performance Lab for personal health assessment. Other hotel facilities include a complete Nautilus center with weights and aerobicycles; tennis, raquetball, and handball courts; a jogging track; aerobics and swimmercise classes; and plenty more, including access to a local country club for golf. *8444 International Dr., Orlando 32819, tel. 407/345–0505 or 800/752–0003. 300 rooms. AE, CB, DC, MC, V. Moderate.*

Sonesta Village Hotel. The Sonesta, located off I–4 near International Drive, is a string of multi-unit townhouses on a lakefront. Following the lead of the all-suite hotels, the Sonesta "villas" consist of small apartments some of which are bilevel with a fully equipped kitchenette, dining room/living room area, small patio, and bedroom. The units are comfortable and homey, each with its private, ground-floor entrance. One bonus of staying at the Sonesta is the outdoor facilities, including tennis courts, mini health club, swimming pool, and whirlpools convenient to each villa. Guests can sail and water-ski on the lake or offer themselves to the sun on a sandy beach. There is a restaurant and bar, but the only action is the nightly outdoor barbecue buffet. If you want to cook at "home" but are too busy to go shopping, the hotel offers a grocery delivery service. Laundry, however, is self-service. *10000 Turkey Lake Rd., Or-*

lando 32819, tel. 407/352–8051 or 800/343–7170. 369 units. AE, DC, MC, V. Expensive.

Stouffer Orlando Resort. From the same people who brought the French bread pizza and Lean Cuisine to the frozen section of your grocery store comes an even more palatable product—the Stouffer Hotel. This first-rate resort was originally the Wyndham Hotel Sea World, until it was sold to the Stouffer chain in 1987. Located directly across the street from Sea World, this bulky, 10-story building looks more like a Federal Reserve Bank than a comfortable hotel. When you enter, you have stepped into what is billed as the largest atrium lobby in the world. Longer than a football field, it takes up the entire core of the building and is ornately landscaped with waterfalls, goldfish ponds, palm trees, glass elevators, and a large, hand-carved, gilded Victorian aviary from Venice, complete with exotic birds.

Facilities include six lighted tennis courts, a swimming pool, a whirlpool, a child-care center, a game room, and access to an 18-hole golf course. On the second floor are a Nautilus-equipped fitness center and a beauty salon where you can work off or hide the effects of dinner in either of two commendable hotel restaurants, *Haifeng* and *Atlantis*. The Stouffer also has its own antiques and gift shops.

It is nice to be greeted with a glass of champagne when you register, but the size of the guest rooms is even more welcoming. They are all large and spacious. The most expensive rooms face the atrium, but if you are a light sleeper, ask for an outside room and avoid the music and party sounds of conventioneers rising through the atrium. *6677 Sea Harbor Dr., Orlando 32821, tel. 407/351–5555 or 800/327–6677. 778 rooms. AE, CB, DC, MC, V. Expensive.*

Maingate Resorts

Maingate refers to an area full of large hotels unaffiliated with Walt Disney World but clustered around its northernmost entrance just off I–4. They are mostly resort hotels on sprawling properties, catering to Walt Disney World vacationers. All are quality hotels with a resort sameness one can find the world over. But in size and price, however, they do vary. As a simple rule of thumb, the bigger the resort and the more extensive the facilities, the more you can expect to pay. If you're looking for a clean, modern room, you cannot go wrong with any of them. All are equally convenient to Walt Disney World, but one may emphasize a particular recreational activity over others. Where you stay may depend on how much time you plan to spend at your hotel or on which stroke—drive or backhand—you feel needs most improving.

Grand Cypress Resort. If you were to ask someone familiar with the Orlando area which resort is the most spectacular, few would hesitate to name the Grand Cypress. The resort property is so extensive—over 1,500 acres—that guests need a trolley system to get around. There is virtually every activity you can imagine at a resort: a dozen tennis courts, boats of all shapes and varieties, scenic bicycling and jogging trails, a full health club, dozens of horses, a 600,000-gallon triple-level swimming pool fed by 12 cascading waterfalls, a 45-acre Audubon nature reserve, 45 holes of Jack Nicklaus–designed golf, and a golfing academy for high-tech analysis of your game.

Guests have a choice of the 750-room Hyatt Regency Grand Cyprus or another 150 rooms at the Villas of Grand Cyprus. The hotel itself is exactly what you would expect from a first-class Hyatt resort, with a 12-story glass atrium filled with tropical plants and classical Asian paintings and sculptures. The rooms are unmemorable but very spacious, and the service is attentive. The best views look out over the pool and the rest of the hotel property. For fine dining, there is *Hemingway's*, specializing in sea food, and *La Coquina*, an upscale French place, both of which are excellent.

This huge resort has just one drawback: the king-size conventions that it commonly attracts. *1 Grand Cypress Blvd., Orlando 32819, tel. 407/239–1234 or 800/228–9000. 750 rooms. AE, DC, MC, V. Very Expensive.*

Hyatt Orlando Hotel. This is another very large hotel, but without the extensive resort facilities. Instead of a single towering building, the hotel consists of 40 two-story buildings in four clusters. Each cluster is a community with its own pool, Jacuzzi, park, and playground at its center. The rooms are spacious, but otherwise unmemorable.

The lobby and convention center are in a building at the center of the clusters. The lobby is vast and mall-like, with numerous shops and restaurants. One of the restaurants, the *Palm Terrace*, features a full kosher menu supervised by the Orthodox Union. There is also a very good take-out deli with great picnic snacks for those wise enough to avoid the lines and prices at amusement park fast-food stands. There are a few tennis courts, but not much else in the way of recreation. However, for busy travelers who will be spending most of their time attacking Orlando's attractions, this is a convenient, not-too-expensive headquarters. *6375 W. Irlo Bronson Memorial Hwy., Kissimmee 32741, tel. 407/396–1234 or 800/228–9000. 946 rooms. AE, CB, DC, MC, V. Moderate.*

Marriott Orlando World Center. To refer to this Marriott as massive would be an understatement. It is the largest hotel in the entire state, with over 1,500 rooms on 28 floors, and luxurious villas, called the Royal Palms and the Sabal Palms, available for weekly rental.

An 18-hole golf course, a dozen tennis courts, a full health club, four swimming pools (one of them the largest in the state), 13 restaurants and bars—this is just the beginning of a list of facilities. The lobby is a huge, opulent atrium, and the rooms are clean and comfortable. The only negative aspects are the overwhelming size and the hundreds of conventioneers. *8701 World Center Dr., Orlando 32821, tel. 407/239–4200 or 800/228–9290. 1,503 rooms. AE, DC, MC, V. Very Expensive.*

★ **Ramada Resort Maingate East at the Park.** The Ramada, with its attractive setting and competitive prices, may offer the best deal in the neighborhood. It has a few tennis courts, a swimming pool with a waterfall, a few shops and restaurants, and a delicatessen for picnickers. The rooms, like the rest of the hotel grounds, are spacious and bright, decked out in tropical and pastel colors. The best rooms, because of the view and light, face the pool. *2900 Parkway Blvd., Kissimmee 32741, tel. 407/*

396–7000, in FL 800/634–4774, or outside FL 800/225–3939. 592 rooms. AE, CB, DC, MC, V. Moderate.

Vistana Resort. Anyone interested in tennis should consider staying at this peaceful resort spread over 50 beautifully landscaped acres. It is also popular with families or groups willing to share a spacious, tastefully decorated villa or town house, each with at least two bedrooms and all the facilities of home—full kitchen, living room, washer/dryer, and so on. The price may seem high, but considering the number of people each condominium-like unit can accommodate (up to six or eight), the rates can be a bargain. The 14 clay and all-weather tennis courts can be used without charge. Private or semiprivate lessons are available for every type of player. Other facilities include a huge free-form swimming pool and a full health club. *13800 Vistana Dr., Lake Buena Vista, 32830, tel. 407/239–3100 or 800/237–9152. 458 units. AE, DC, MC, V. Very Expensive.*

U.S. 192 Area

If you are looking for anything remotely quaint, charming, or sophisticated, move on. The U.S. 192 strip, formally called Irlo Bronson Memorial Highway and referred to as the Spacecoast Parkway, is generally known as Kissimmee; but whatever you call it, it is an avenue crammed with bargain basement motels, hotels, cheap restaurants, fast-food chains, nickel and dime attractions, gas stations, and mini-marts. If all you are looking for is a decent room with perhaps a few extras for a manageable price, this is your wonderland. The number of motels here is mind-boggling. It is a buyer's market, and room rates start as low as $20 a night—or lower if it is the right time of year and you can cut the right deal. But most rooms will run about $30–$70 a night, depending on the hotel's facilities and its proximity to Disney World. Among the chain hotels—Travelodge, Econolodge, Comfort Inn, Holiday Inn, Radisson, Sheraton, Best Western, and so on—are a pride of family-operated motels, many of which are run by recent immigrants: a Norwegian couple at the Viking Motel, say, or a Chinese family at the Casa Rosa.

The rooms are very basic and there is not a whole lot of difference between them. As a rule, the newer the property, the more comfortable your surroundings are likely to be. Also, the farther you are from Disney World, the lower the rates; a few minutes' drive may save you a significant amount of money. As you drive through Kissimmee, shop around for what appeals to you. Don't be bashful about going up to a registration desk and asking to see a room before you make a decision.

Casa Rosa Inn. For simple motel living—no screaming kids or loud music, please—this is your place. The pink, Spanish-style motel does not have much in the way of facilities other than a little swimming pool and free in-room movies, but it is a good, serviceable place to hang your hat. *4600 W. Irlo Bronson Memorial Hwy., Kissimmee 32741, tel. 407/396–2020 or 800/874–1589. 50 rooms. AE, MC, V. Inexpensive.*

Cedar Lakeside Inn. Just a few doors down from the Travelodge is another adequate bargain hotel. The Mediterranean-style motel architecture is not likely to charm you off your feet, but the staff is friendly and facilities include a swimming pool, a Jacuzzi, and a lakefront beach with picnic areas, waterskiing, sailing, and paddleboats. Ask for a room as close to the lake as possible. Since there's no restaurant, you may want to pay an extra $10 for a room with a kitchenette. *4960 W. Irlo Bronson Memorial Hwy., Kissimmee 32741, tel. 407/396–1376 or 800/ 327–0072. 200 rooms. AE, CB, DC, MC, V. Inexpensive.*

Radisson Inn Maingate. This is the one of the newest hotels on the strip, located just a few minutes from WDW's front door. It is a very sleek, modern building with cheerful guest rooms, large bathrooms, and plenty of extras for the price. Facilities include a swimming pool, a whirlpool, a few tennis courts, and a jogging trail. Not fancy, but sufficient. The best rooms are those with a view of the pool. One floor is reserved for nonsmokers. *7501 W. Irlo Bronson Memorial Hwy., Kissimmee 32741, tel. 407/396–1400 or 800/333–3333. 580 rooms. AE, CB, DC, MC, V. Moderate.*

The Residence Inn. Of the all-suite hotels on U.S. 192, this one is probably the best. It consists of a row of four-unit town houses with private stairway entrances to each suite. One side of the unit faces the highway, the other overlooks a rather attractive lake, where visitors can sail, waterski, jet-ski, and fish. Forty of the units are penthouses, with complete kitchens, small living rooms, loft bedrooms, and even fireplaces. The other units are set up like studio apartments, but still contain full kitchens and fireplaces. Regular studio suites accommodate two people; double studios accommodate up to four. Both Continental breakfast and a grocery shopping service are complimentary. The price may seem expensive, considering the location, but there is no charge for additional guests, so you can squeeze in the whole family at no extra cost. *4786 W. Irlo Bronson Memorial Hwy., Kissimmee 32741, tel. 407/396–2056 or 800/468–3027. 160 units. AE, CB, DC, MC, V. Moderate– Expensive.*

Sheraton Lakeside Inn. This is a comfortable but undistinguished resort-style hotel, offering quite a few recreational facilities for its price. The complex consists of 15 two-story buildings spread over 25 acres. Facilities include heated pools, wading pools for tots, paddleboats, 18 holes of miniature golf, and 4 tennis courts. There is also a seafood restaurant, a deli, and a bar. *7711 W. Irlo Bronson Memorial Hwy., Kissimmee 32741, tel. 407/828–8250 or 800/325–3535. 652 rooms. AE, CB, DC, MC, V. Moderate.*

Travelodge Golden Triangle. The surroundings are less than ideal, but the price is right for a clean room in a new hotel with a pool and a small sandy beach. There is a bar/restaurant in the lobby and there are a few decent, inexpensive restaurants in the neighborhood. The hotel sits between the highway and a lake with paddleboards, sailing, jet-skis, and waterskiing. No room has much of a view, but try to get one as close to the lake as possible to avoid highway noise. *4944 W. Irlo Bronson Memorial Hwy., Kissimmee 32741, tel. 407/396–4455 or 800/228– 4427. 222 rooms. AE, CB, DC, MC, V. Inexpensive.*

Off the Beaten Track

Winter Park

Mention should be made of two hotels that are off the beaten track—close enough to be part of the immediate Orlando area, but not so close that they fit into one of our categories.

★ **Park Plaza Hotel.** Located in Orlando's very posh, established neighborhood of Winter Park, the Park Plaza is an old-fashioned wood and wicker Southern hotel, built in 1922. If you are in need of recreational facilities or special amenities, look elsewhere, but if you are hoping to find real Southern charm and hospitality, this is perhaps the best place in the Orlando area to find it. You are as far from the world of tourism as you can get and still within a short driving distance of all the major attractions. It is a small, intimate hotel that gives you the feeling that you are a guest in somebody's home. You wake up in the morning to a newspaper under your door, for example.

All of the rooms open up onto one long balcony, covered with ferns, flowers, and wicker furniture. Rooms have either one double- or queen-size bed, and come in various sizes, with views of Park Avenue or Central Park. On the first floor is one of Orlando's most popular restaurants, the *Park Plaza Gardens*, where over Continental cuisine you can see-and-be-seen by the fashionable folk of Winter Park. *307 Park Ave. S, Winter Park 32789, tel. 407/647–1072 or 800/228–7220. 27 rooms. AE, CB, DC, MC, V. Moderate–Expensive. To get there, drive east on I–4 and exit at Fairbanks Ave. Turn right for 1 mi until you reach Park Ave. The hotel is on your left.*

Lake Wales

★ **Chalet Suzanne.** You'll find this conversation-piece of a hotel in orange grove territory, in what seems the middle of nowhere. A homemade billboard directs you down a country road that turns into a palm-lined drive. Cobblestone paths lead to a row of chalet-style houses and cabins, complete with balconies and thatched roofing. On one side are fields and gardens, on the other, a lake.

The Chalet Suzanne is a friendly, homespun mom and pop operation. It has been in the Hinshaw family for generations and was turned into a country inn when family fortunes dwindled in the 1930s. The inn has been built bit-by-unlikely-bit over the years, and the furnishings range from the rare and valuable to the garage sale special. The grounds are decorated with colorful tilework from Portugal, ironwork from Spain, pottery from Italy, and porcelain from England and Germany.

Each room has its own personality, as in the house of a rich, eccentric old uncle. Bathrooms are tiled and have old-fashioned tubs and wash basins. The most charming rooms face the lake. *U.S. 27S, Drawer AC, Lake Wales 33859, tel. 813/676–6011. 30 rooms. AE, CB, DC, MC, V. Moderate–Expensive. To get there, either land your Cessna or Lear jet on their private airstrip, or drive. Go west on I–4 from Orlando to the Rte. 27 exit and head toward Cypress Gardens. The Chalet's billboard is past the Cypress Gardens turnoff, just after Lake Wales.*

9 Nightlife

Disney World Dinner Shows

Broadway at the Top. This is Disney's sophisticated nighttime entertainment spot, located at the top of the World Nightclub atop the Contemporary Resort. The spirited show runs for about an hour after each of the two nightly seatings for dinner. A cast of high-energy dancers and singers brings to life some of Broadway's greatest hits. A single price includes the show and dinner. Tax, gratuity, and alcoholic drinks are extra. *Contemporary Resort, tel. 407/W–DISNEY. Reservations necessary months in advance. Jackets required. Admission: $40 adults, $15 children 3–11. Seatings at 6 PM and 9:15 PM.*

Polynesian Revue and Mickey's Tropical Revue. Put on some comfortable, casual clothes and head over to the Polynesian Village Resort for an outdoor barbecue and a tropical Luau complete with fire jugglers and hula drum dancers. It's a colorful, South Pacific setting and an easy-going evening that families find relaxing and trouble-free. There are two shows nightly of the Polynesian Revue and an earlier show for children called Mickey's Tropical Revue, where Disney characters perform decked out in costumes befitting these South Seas surroundings. *Polynesian Village Resort, tel. 407/W–DISNEY. Dress: casual. Reservations necessary, usually months in advance. Polynesian Review: $28 adults, $23 juniors 12–20, and $15 children 3–11. Seatings at 6:45 PM and 9:30 PM. Mickey's Tropical Revue: $24.50 adults, $19.50 juniors, $11 children. Seating at 4:30 PM.*

Hoop-Dee-Doo Revue. This family-entertainment dinner show may be corny but it is also the liveliest and most rollicking in Walt Disney World. A troupe of jokers called the Pioneer Hall Players stomp their feet, wisecrack, and make merry in this Western mess-hall setting. The chow consists of barbecued ribs, fried chicken, corn-on-the-cob, strawberry shortcake, and all the fixin's. There are three shows nightly at Pioneer Hall in Fort Wilderness area—not always the easiest place to get to. *Fort Wilderness Resort, tel. 407/W–DISNEY. Dress: informal. Reservations necessary, usually months in advance. Admission: $29 adults, $23 juniors 12–20, $15 children 3–11. Seatings at 5, 7:30, and 10 PM.*

Pleasure Island. There is a single admission charge to this nightlife entertainment complex, which features a comedy club, teenage dance center, rock n' roller skating rink disco, numerous restaurants, lounges, shops, and even a 10-screen theater complex. Six themed nightclubs offer everything from swinging jazz to foot stompin' country-and-western to the latest pop video hits. Every night is a Saturday night in this action-packed theme park.

IllumiNations. You won't want to miss Epcot's grand finale, a laser show that takes place every night just before Epcot closes, along the shores of the World Showcase lagoon. It is a show unlike any other. In the middle of the lagoon, laser projections of dancing images move across screens of spraying water. Orchestral music fills the air as multicolored neon lasers streak across the sky, pulsating to the rhythms of the music. Suddenly the night lights up with brilliant fireworks, lasers play over the low-hanging smoke, and the air vibrates with the sounds of Tchaikovsky's *1812 Overture*. Projections of the Earth's continents transform Spaceship Earth into a luminescent, spinning globe. With this dramatic finale, the crowds exit as Spaceship Earth continues to "rotate." The lasers used to create these images are powerful enough to project an identical image on a golf ball up to five miles away. It is a stellar performance that you won't want to miss.

Some places around the lagoon offer much better vantage points than others for watching the laser show. The best locations are the Matsu No Ma Lounge in the Japan Pavilion, the patios of the Rose and Crown in the United Kingdom Pavilion, and Cantina de San Angel in the Mexican Pavilion. Another good spot is the World Showcase Plaza between the boat docks at the Showcase entrance, but this is often crowded with visitors who want to make a quick dash homeward after the show; if you want to join them there, claim your seat at least an hour in advance. Since the fireworks create a good deal of smoke, you will not want to be downwind of it, so use the old lick-the-finger test to see which way the wind is blowing, and position yourself accordingly.

The Orlando Area

Until a few years ago, Orlando's nightlife was more like that of Oskaloosa, Iowa, than of a booming tourist haven. But slowly, an after-dark scene has developed, spreading farther and farther beyond the realm of Disney. Orlando entrepreneurs have now caught on that there is a fortune to be had satisfying the fun-hungry night owls who flock to this city. New night spots are opening constantly—everything from flashy discos to ballroom dancing, salons, country-and-western saloons, Broadway dinner theaters, even medieval jousting tournaments.

The Arts

If all the fantasy starts to wear thin and you feel the need for more sophisticated entertainment, check out the local fine arts scene in the "Happenings" and "Calendar" sections of *Orlando Magazine*, or *Center Stage*, available at any newsstand. The average price of a ticket to performing arts events in the Orlando area rarely exceeds $10–$12, and is often half that price.

Orlando has an active performing arts agenda of ballet, modern dance, classical music, opera, and theater, much of which takes place at the **Carr Performing Arts Centre** (401 Livingston St., Orlando, tel. 407/896–7365). This community auditorium presents a different play each month (Wed. through Sat., with Sun. matinees). The Broadway series features performances on the way to Broadway or current road shows.

During the school year, **Rollins College** (tel. 407/646–2233) in Winter Park has a choral and symphonic concert series which is open to the public and usually free. The first week of March there is a **Bach Music Festival** (tel. 407/646–2182) that has been a Winter Park tradition for over 55 years. Also at the college is the **Annie Russell Theater** (tel. 407/646–2501), which has a regular series of productions.

Across the street from the Peabody Hotel on International Drive is the **Orange County Civic and Convention Center** (tel. 407/345–9898) which hosts many big-name performing artists.

Dinner Shows

Dinner shows have become an immensely popular form of nighttime entertainment around Orlando. A set price usually buys a multiple-course dinner and a theatrical production—a totally escapist experience. The food tends to be predictable—definitely not the major attraction. Always call and make reservations in advance, especially on weekends. A lively crowd can be an asset; a show playing to a small audience can be a pathetic and embarrassing sight. What the shows lack in substance and depth they make up for in color and enthusiasm. The result is an evening of light entertainment, which kids in particular will enjoy.

Arabian Nights. This attraction features 60 performing horses, music, special effects, a chariot race, and a four-course dinner. *6225 W. Irlo Bronson Memorial Hwy. (U.S. 192), Kissimmee, tel. 407/351–5822 or 800/553–6116. Dress: casual. Reservations necessary. All major credit cards. Admission: $24 adults, $16 children 3–11.*

Mardi Gras. This jazzy, New Orleans–style show is the best of Orlando's dinner attractions. The set menu consists of mixed vegetable soup, tossed salad, buckets of fried chicken, platters of roast beef, apple pie with ice cream, and all the beer, wine, or soda you can drink. It is not an elaborate meal, but it is as good as one can expect from a dinner theater. A New Orleans jazz band plays during dinner, followed by a one-hour cabaret with colorful song and dance routines to rhythms of the Caribbean, Latin America, and Dixieland jazz. Although the kids are more likely to vote for the Wild West or medieval shows, adults tend to prefer Mardi Gras because it is more of a restaurant nightclub than a fantasyland. *At the Mercado Shopping Village, 8445 International Dr., Orlando, tel. 407/351–5151 or 800/641–5151. Dress: casual. Reservations necessary. All major credit cards. Admission: $23.95 adults, $15.95 children 3–11.*

Fort Liberty. Run by the same company that operates Mardi Gras and King Henry's Feast, this dinner show whisks you out to the Wild West, back to the days of cowboys and Indians. The entertainment is a mixed bag of real Indian dances, foot stompin' singalongs, and acrobatics. A British cowboy shows what he can do with bullwhips and lassoes, and a musician plays the *1812 Overture* on the tuba and *America the Beautiful* on an old saw (yes, the kind that cuts wood). The show is full of slapstick theatrics and country western shindigging that children really enjoy. The chow is what you might expect to eat with John Wayne out on the prairie: beef soup, fried chicken, corn-on-the-cob, and, of course, the food that won the West—pork and beans. You are served by a rowdy chorus of cavalry recruits who keep the food coming and beverages freely pouring. All tables seat 12, so unless you are in a big party, expect to develop pass-the-ketchup relationships.

Fort Liberty is a stockade filled with shops and stalls selling Western-themed gifts and souvenirs. The ambiance is set by the photographers snapping photos of visitors dressed in cowboy garb. Forever trying to attract tourists, the Fort Liberty entertainers perform in the courtyard during the day. If the kids are more intent on seeing Marlboro Country than you are, go at lunch time (11–2), pick up some fast-food fried chicken for

$2 and see many of the acts that are in the dinner show. *5260 W. Irlo Bronson Memorial Hwy. (U.S. 192), Kissimmee, tel. 407/ 351–5151 or 800/641–5151. Dress: casual. Reservations necessary. AE, DC, MC, V. Admission: $23.95 adults, $15.95 children 3–11.*

King Henry's Feast. Driving along the strip of hotels and shopping malls on I–4 or International Drive, you may notice two Tudor-style buildings. One of them is the Econolodge, the other is the home of Orlando's King Henry VIII and his court of 16th-century jesters. The entertainment includes a corny but talented magician, a daring fire-swallowing acrobat, and much singing, dancing, and revelry as King Henry celebrates his birthday and begins his quest for his seventh bride.

Saucy wenches, who refer to customers as "me lords" and "me ladies," serve potato leek soup, salad, chicken and ribs, and all the beer, wine, and soft drinks you can guzzle. Bar drinks are extra. *8984 International Dr., Orlando, tel. 407/351–5151 or 800/641–5151. Dress: casual. Reservations necessary. AE, DC, MC, V. Admission: $23.95 adults, $15.95 children 3–11.*

Medieval Times. In a huge, modern-medieval manor house, visitors enjoy a four-course dinner while watching the struggle of good and evil in a tournament of games, sword fights, and jousting matches, including no less than 30 charging horses and a cast of 75 knights, nobles, and maidens. Sounds silly? It is. Yet if you view it through the eyes of your children, this two-hour extravaganza of pageantry and meat-and-potatoes banquet fare can be an amusing event.

Everyone faces forward along narrow banquet tables that are stepped auditorium-style above the tournament. If you and your family traveled the amusement park route all day and are tired of looking at or nagging at each other, you may get some respite, a bit of comic relief, and possibly some vicarious pleasure from a night of crossing lances. *4510 W. Irlo Bronson Memorial Hwy. (U.S. 192), Kissimmee, tel. 407/239–0214 or 407/396–1518, in FL 800/432–0768, outside FL 800/327–4024. Dress: informal. Reservations necessary. AE, MC, V. $25 adults, $17 children 3–12.*

Bavarian Schnitzel House. If you have any interest in German food, this funloving place serves the area's finest. The Red Baron would feel right at home in this kitschy Bavarian world, which none of the rowdy revellers seems to mind. The entertainment is a five-piece oompah band that shakes, rattles, and groans at its own corny jokes. They do a good job of getting the audience to sing, dance, and laugh the night away. Go on a crowded weekend night; if you're going to succumb, you may as well go all the way. There is no cover charge for the entertainment, and dinner is à la carte. Meals are hearty and not very expensive. Goulash soup, wiener schnitzel, and a few steins of German beer ought to set you up for a jovial evening. *6159 Westwood Blvd. (just off International Dr.), Orlando, tel. 407/ 352–8484. Dress: casual. Reservations suggested. AE, DC, MC, V. Inexpensive–Moderate.*

Mark Two. This is the only true dinner theater in Orlando, with full Broadway musicals such as *Oklahoma, My Fair Lady, West Side Story*, and *South Pacific* staged through most of the year. During the Christmas holiday season, shorter Broadway musical revues are presented.

A buffet and full-service cocktail bar is open for business 90 minutes before the show. The food is nothing to write home about and should not be the reason to pay a visit. The buffet of seafood Newburg, baked whitefish, a variety of meats, and salad bar is only a few notches above cafeteria food. Best bets are the rich desserts that arrive during intermission.

The shows are directed by the theater's owner, and the sets, costumes, music, and choreography are all done in-house. The actors are mostly from the Orlando area. It will not be the best performance you will ever see, but it can be a pleasure to hear the scores and see the routines of a favorite old musical while you are sitting comfortably at your table with a drink in hand. Each show runs for about six weeks, so call to see what will be playing while you are in town. There are eight shows a week, including matinees. The cost of the show, including your meal, ranges from $20 to $24 for adults and $15–$19 for children (12 and under). The buffet is served from 6:30 to 7:30 PM. Performance starts at 8 PM. *Edgewater Center, 3376 Edgewater Dr., Orlando (from I–4 take Exit 44 and go west), tel. 407/843–6275. Dress: casual. Reservations suggested. AE, MC, V. Closed Mon. Moderate.*

Church Street Station

This downtown Orlando attraction is a complete entertainment experience. Widely popular among both tourists and locals, it single-handedly began downtown Orlando's metamorphosis from a sleepy town to the nighttime hotspot it now boasts to be, and is on its way to becoming.

Until the early 1970s, Church Street offered nothing more than a dilapidated hotel, a few lifeless buildings, and a tired old train station. Attempting to convert this run-down neighborhood into a trendy entertainment complex was quite an ambitious venture.

What today is a vast complex of old fashioned saloons, dance halls, dining rooms, and shopping arcades began with just one bar—**Rosie O'Grady's**. As Rosie's popularity increased over the years, developer/owner Bob Snow acquired a neighboring building, and the complex began to spread. Now, both sides of the block are dazzlingly restored. Unlike much of what you see in Disney World, this place doesn't just look authentic—it *is* authentic. The train on the tracks is an actual 19th-century steam engine; the whistling calliope was especially rebuilt to blow its original tunes. Just about everything down to the cobblestones that clatter under the horse-drawn carriages are the real McCoy. Buildings have been completely redecorated with collectibles and memorabilia from around the world; look carefully at the details and don't be shy about asking where something came from. You may be surprised to discover that a beautiful mahogany phone booth is actually a confessional that was salvaged from a French monastery.

You can spend an evening in part of the complex, or you can wander from area to area, soaking up the peculiar characteristics of each. For a single admission price of $14.95 (adults) or $8.95 (4–12), you're permitted to wander freely, stay as long as you wish, and do what you want, whether it's drinking, dancing, dining, or people-watching. Food and drink cost extra and are not cheap, but they add to the fun. Parts of the complex are open during the day, but the place is usually quiet then; the pace picks up at night, especially on weekends, with crowds thickest from 10 to 11. The streets can get insanely busy at these times, but it's all part of the spirit of bustling good fun that continues into the night. *129 W. Church St., Orlando, tel. 407/422–2434. Reservations not necessary. Dress: casual. AE, MC, V.*

Rosie O'Grady's. This is a turn-of-the-century saloon with dark wood, brass trim, a full Dixieland band blaring out of a gazebo, counter top can-can dancers, tap dancers, and vaudeville singers. Is this a set for *The Music Man* or an evening at the Moulin Rouge? It's difficult at first to tell. The 90-minute shows begin at 7 or 7:30 PM. The last show starts at 11:45. Multidecker sandwiches and hot dogs are sold in the Gay 90s Sandwich Parlour from 4:30 PM till 11 PM.

Apple Annie's Courtyard. This is a relatively quiet—some would say flairless—nook that features continuous live folk and bluegrass music from about 8 PM to 2 AM. It's a good place to rest your feet, have a drink, and people-watch. Salads, fruit platters, and exotic drinks are served from 11 AM to 2 AM.

Lili Marlene's Aviator Pub. Here you have a relaxed, wood-paneled English pub atmosphere and the finest dining on Church Street. Food is hearty, upscale, and very American—mostly steaks, ribs, and seafood. Prices are not cheap. The walls have biplane-era memorabilia, and a large-scale model aircraft hangs from the ceiling. Open for lunch and dinner until midnight.

Phineas Phogg's Balloon Works. This is a very popular happening disco filled with young singles over 21 and a sprinkling of old-timers showing off their moves on the dance floor. It has a good-looking yuppie tourist crowd, leavened with locals. Contemporary dance tunes are played on a sound system that will blow your argyle socks off. The place is jammed by midnight and open until 2. Much of the young crowd feels it is worth the price of admission into the Station just to be able to come here.

Orchid Garden. Decorative lamps, iron latticework, arched ceilings, and stained-glass windows create a striking Victorian arcade where visitors sit, drink, and listen to a first-rate band pounding out popular tunes from the 1950s to the '80s. Open until 2 AM.

Cracker's Raw Bar. Located behind the Orchid Garden, Cracker's is a good place to get a quick gumbo or chowder fix and slam down a few oysters with a beer chaser. Open until midnight.

Cheyenne Saloon. This is the biggest, fanciest, rootin'-tootin' saloon you may ever see. The former triple-level opera house is covered with moose racks, steer horns, buffalo heads, and Remington rifles; and there is a seven-piece country-western band that darn near brings the house down. This is a fun crowd to watch with all the pickin', strummin', fiddlin', hollerin', and do-see-doin'. Make sure you come equipped with your best stompin' shoes, cowboy hat, and catcalls. An upstairs restaurant serves chicken-and-ribs saloon fare. The shows start at 7:30, 11, and 12:45 AM.

Church Street Station Exchange. The newest addition to the complex, near Church Street Station, is a razzle-dazzle marketplace filled with all sorts of specialty shops and old-fashioned theme restaurants.

Bars and Clubs

The bars and nightclubs have been divided into two sections. The first covers the tourist hotel districts in the Disney area, including Kissimmee, Lake Buena Vista, and International Drive. These places are usually filled with visitors to Walt Disney World. The other section covers the city of Orlando and Winter Park, both of which cater to a more local crowd. Remember that clubs on Disney property are allowed to stay open later than bars elsewhere, and many of them don't have last call until 2:45 AM.

Disney Area   **Little Darlin's Rock n' Roll Palace.** Shake, rattle, and roll the night away in this 1950s and '60s nostalgia nightclub. The interior looks like an opera house, and there's an orchestra pit dance floor and a huge bandstand stage featuring famous old rock bands that still tour, such as The Drifters and The Platters. The crowd is a mix of young and old, singles and couples. The club features a very talented house band that serves up live music seven nights a week. The menu is vintage '50s: Philly hot dogs, cheese steak sandwiches, banana splits, and, for some strange reason, escargots. *Old Town, 5770 Spacecoast Pkwy., Kissimmee 32741, tel. 407/396–6499. Dress: casual. Admission: $6.95 adults, $3.50 children under 8.*

Giraffe Lounge. Located inside the Hotel Royal Plaza in WDW Village at Lake Buena Vista, this flashy disco with spinning, colored lights is usually densely packed on weekends. It is a small place, and classy it ain't, but there's a lot going on, including live bands five nights a week. Happy hour runs daily from 4 to 9:30 PM. Music plays and the bartender pours until 3 AM. *Hotel Royal Plaza, WDW Village, Lake Buena Vista, tel. 407/828–2828. Dress: casual. Open 4 PM–3 AM. No cover charge.*

The Laughing Kookaburra. A big hotel disco with live band music nightly and a serious singles crowd of all ages. The music is loud and the dance floor can get very crowded—a plus for some, a minus for others. The bar serves up 99 brands of beer, plus cocktails. Happy hour with free bar food runs daily from 4 to 8 PM. The band plays six nights a week (off Mon.). *Buena Vista Palace Hotel, WDW Village, Lake Buena Vista, tel. 407/827–2727. Dress: casual. All major credit cards. Open 4 PM–3 AM. No cover charge.*

La Cantina. This little bar in the Hotel Royal Plaza has guitar music seven days a week and a happy hour Sunday through Thursday, midnight until 3 AM! Good thing most visitors are hotel guests—it's hard to get in an accident in an elevator! *Hotel Royal Plaza, tel. 407/828–2828. Open 11 AM–3 AM.*

Top of the Tower. Listen to a comedian tell jokes and play country and rock n' roll classics on the guitar while you check out a tremendous view of Disney World. A very comfy hotel bar with a nice tame bunch of people. *Viscount Hotel, tel. 407/828–2424. Dress: casual. Open 8:30 PM–3 AM. No cover charge.*

Bennigan's. A young singles spot that draws crowds in the early evening and during happy hours from 4 to 7 PM and from 11 PM to 2 AM. It caters mostly to nontourists who work in the area.

Food is served almost until closing. *6324 International Dr., Orlando, tel. 407/351–4436. Open 11 AM–2 AM.*

Orlando Area The nightclubs in Orlando have significantly more character than those in the Disney hotel area. If you have the energy to get in your car, you will probably find these spots more satisfying and less touristy—if you can find them.

J.J. Whispers. A classy, brassy singles crowd flocks to this trendy disco, which tries hard to maintain an image of cosmopolitan class. Expect to mingle with fashion-conscious locals in their tastefully outrageous attire. The club is equally popular with the over-30 set, who listen to music from the 1940s, '50s, and '60s in the Showroom. The young people do what young people do in a massive, multilevel, state-of-the-art disco. J.J.'s has one restaurant serving bar-food fare, and another, a deli, that is open for lunch and sometimes features comedians, magicians, and other stage acts. Live entertainment (Tues.–Sun., 8 PM–2 AM) includes all-male and all-female revues and live bands. *5100 Adanson St., Orlando, tel. 407/629–4779. Dress: tasteful but outrageous—or just a jacket. AE, MC, V. Cover: $2 and up. To get there, take I–4 to the Lee Rd. exit and go west for about ½ mi on Lee Rd. Watch for a sharp left-hand turn at Adanson St. J.J.'s is located at the end of the Lee Rd. Shopping Center.*

Cheek-to-Cheek. Monday nights are a big deal here because of the many big-name performers—mostly contemporary jazz musicians in the Class Act Lounge, and rock and reggae in Cheek-to-Cheek. Past performers include Al Stewart, Wynton Marsalis, Rita Coolidge, and even Tommy Dorsey. The place can get very crowded, with tables crammed so close together that you will become fast friends, or enemies, with your neighbors. Other nights of the week (Tues.–Sat.) are very popular with the 35–50-year-old crowd who dance to Top 40s music played by Cheek-to-Cheek's house band. *839 N. Orlando Ave. (U.S. 17–92), tel. 407/644–2060. Open 8 PM–2 AM. Concert admission Mon. up to $20; cover charge Tues.–Thurs. $3 (ladies free), Fri. and Sat. $4. Closed some Sun.*

Crocodile Club. This bar, inside a restaurant called Bailey's in Winter Park, collects a young, well-dressed college crowd from neighboring Rollins College. The atmosphere is more sophisticated and yuppified than most Orlando bars. Expect to hear Motown and dance to pop. *Bailey's Restaurant, 118 W. Fairbanks Ave., Winter Park, tel. 407/647–8501.*

Sullivan's Trailways Lounge. A very popular place with much right-friendly charm where people of all ages and many families come to strut their stuff on the largest dance floor in Florida. Even Yankees are welcome in this Southern country-western dance hall. Big name performers entertain on occasion; local bands play nightly except Sunday. *1108 S. Orange Blossom Trail (U.S. 441), tel. 407/843–2934. Bands play 9 PM–2 AM. Cover charge: $2 and up.*

Index

Index

Personal Itinerary

Departure *Date*

Time

Transportation

Arrival *Date*   *Time*

Departure *Date*   *Time*

Transportation

Accommodations

Arrival *Date*   *Time*

Departure *Date*   *Time*

Transportation

Accommodations

Arrival *Date*   *Time*

Departure *Date*   *Time*

Transportation

Accommodations

Personal Itinerary

Arrival *Date*   *Time*

Departure *Date*   *Time*

Transportation

Accommodations

Arrival *Date*   *Time*

Departure *Date*   *Time*

Transportation

Accommodations

Arrival *Date*   *Time*

Departure *Date*   *Time*

Transportation

Accommodations

Arrival *Date*   *Time*

Departure *Date*   *Time*

Transportation

Accommodations

Personal Itinerary

Arrival *Date*   *Time*

Departure *Date*   *Time*

Transportation

Accommodations

Arrival *Date*   *Time*

Departure *Date*   *Time*

Transportation

Accommodations

Arrival *Date*   *Time*

Departure *Date*   *Time*

Transportation

Accommodations

Arrival *Date*   *Time*

Departure *Date*   *Time*

Transportation

Accommodations

Personal Itinerary

Arrival *Date*   *Time*

Departure *Date*   *Time*

Transportation

Accommodations

Arrival *Date*   *Time*

Departure *Date*   *Time*

Transportation

Accommodations

Arrival *Date*   *Time*

Departure *Date*   *Time*

Transportation

Accommodations

Arrival *Date*   *Time*

Departure *Date*   *Time*

Transportation

Accommodations

Personal Itinerary

Arrival *Date*   *Time*

Departure *Date*   *Time*

Transportation

Accommodations

Arrival *Date*   *Time*

Departure *Date*   *Time*

Transportation

Accommodations

Arrival *Date*   *Time*

Departure *Date*   *Time*

Transportation

Accommodations

Arrival *Date*   *Time*

Departure *Date*   *Time*

Transportation

Accommodations

Personal Itinerary

Arrival *Date*   *Time*

Departure *Date*   *Time*

Transportation

Accommodations

Arrival *Date*   *Time*

Departure *Date*   *Time*

Transportation

Accommodations

Arrival *Date*   *Time*

Departure *Date*   *Time*

Transportation

Accommodations

Arrival *Date*   *Time*

Departure *Date*   *Time*

Transportation

Accommodations

Addresses

Name	*Name*
Address	*Address*
Telephone	*Telephone*
Name	*Name*
Address	*Address*
Telephone	*Telephone*
Name	*Name*
Address	*Address*
Telephone	*Telephone*
Name	*Name*
Address	*Address*
Telephone	*Telephone*
Name	*Name*
Address	*Address*
Telephone	*Telephone*
Name	*Name*
Address	*Address*
Telephone	*Telephone*
Name	*Name*
Address	*Address*
Telephone	*Telephone*
Name	*Name*
Address	*Address*
Telephone	*Telephone*

Addresses

Name | *Name*

Address | *Address*

Telephone | *Telephone*

Name | *Name*

Address | *Address*

Telephone | *Telephone*

Name | *Name*

Address | *Address*

Telephone | *Telephone*

Name | *Name*

Address | *Address*

Telephone | *Telephone*

Name | *Name*

Address | *Address*

Telephone | *Telephone*

Name | *Name*

Address | *Address*

Telephone | *Telephone*

Name | *Name*

Address | *Address*

Telephone | *Telephone*

Name | *Name*

Address | *Address*

Telephone | *Telephone*

Addresses

Name	*Name*
Address	*Address*
Telephone	*Telephone*
Name	*Name*
Address	*Address*
Telephone	*Telephone*
Name	*Name*
Address	*Address*
Telephone	*Telephone*
Name	*Name*
Address	*Address*
Telephone	*Telephone*
Name	*Name*
Address	*Address*
Telephone	*Telephone*
Name	*Name*
Address	*Address*
Telephone	*Telephone*
Name	*Name*
Address	*Address*
Telephone	*Telephone*
Name	*Name*
Address	*Address*
Telephone	*Telephone*

Fodor's Travel Guides

U.S. Guides

Alaska
Arizona
Atlantic City & the
  New Jersey Shore
Boston
California
Cape Cod
Carolinas & the
  Georgia Coast
The Chesapeake Region
Chicago
Colorado
Dallas & Fort
  Worth

Disney World & the
  Orlando Area
Florida
Hawaii
Houston &
  Galveston
Las Vegas
Los Angeles, Orange
  County, Palm Springs
Maui
Miami, Fort Lauderdale,
  Palm Beach
Michigan, Wisconsin,
  Minnesota

New England
New Mexico
New Orleans
New Orleans (Pocket
  Guide)
New York City
New York City (Pocket
  Guide)
New York State
Pacific North Coast
Philadelphia
The Rockies
San Diego
San Francisco

San Francisco (Pocket
  Guide)
The South
Texas
USA
Virgin Islands
Virginia
Waikiki
Washington, DC
Williamsburg

Foreign Guides

Acapulco
Amsterdam
Australia, New Zealand,
  The South Pacific
Austria
Bahamas
Bahamas (Pocket
  Guide)
Baja & the Pacific
  Coast Resorts
Barbados
Belgium & Luxembourg
Bermuda
Brazil
Britain (Great Travel
  Values)
Budget Europe
Canada
Canada (Great Travel
  Values)
Canada's Atlantic
  Provinces
Cancún, Cozumel,
  Mérida, the
  Yucatán
Caribbean

Caribbean (Great
  Travel Values)
Central America
China
China's Great Cities
Eastern Europe
Egypt
Europe
Europe's Great Cities
Florence & Venice
France
France (Great Travel
  Values)
Germany
Germany (Great Travel
  Values)
Great Britain
Greece
The Himalayan
  Countries
Holland
Hong Kong
Hungary
India, including Nepal
Ireland
Israel

Italy
Italy (Great Travel
  Values)
Jamaica
Japan
Japan (Great Travel
  Values)
Jordan & the Holy Land
Kenya, Tanzania,
  the Seychelles
Korea
Lisbon
Loire Valley
London
London (Great Travel
  Values)
London (Pocket Guide)
Madrid & Barcelona
Mexico
Mexico City
Montreal &
  Quebec City
Munich
New Zealand
North Africa
Paris

Paris (Pocket Guide)
Portugal
Rio de Janeiro
The Riviera (Fun on)
Rome
Saint Martin &
  Sint Maarten
Scandinavia
Scandinavian Cities
Scotland
Singapore
South America
South Pacific
Southeast Asia
Soviet Union
Spain
Spain (Great Travel
  Values)
Sweden
Switzerland
Sydney
Tokyo
Toronto
Turkey
Vienna
Yugoslavia

Special-Interest Guides

Bed & Breakfast
  Guide: North America
Health & Fitness
  Vacations

Royalty Watching
Selected Hotels of
  Europe

Selected Resorts
  and Hotels of the U.S.
Shopping in Europe

Skiing in North
  America
Sunday in New York

*Help us evaluate hotels and restaurants
for the next edition of this guide, and
we will send you a free issue of Fodor's
newsletter, TravelSense.*

Title of this guide:

1 Hotel ❑   Restaurant ❑   *(check one)*

Name

Number/Street

City/State/Country

Comments

2 Hotel ❑   Restaurant ❑   *(check one)*

Name

Number/Street

City/State/Country

Comments

3 Hotel ❑   Restaurant ❑   *(check one)*

Name

Number/Street

City/State/Country

Comments

General Comments

Please complete for a free copy of TravelSense

Name

Number/Street

City/State/Zip

Business Reply Mail

First Class   Permit Nº 7775   New York, NY

Postage will be paid by addressee

Fodor's Travel Publications

201 East 50th Street

New York, NY 10022